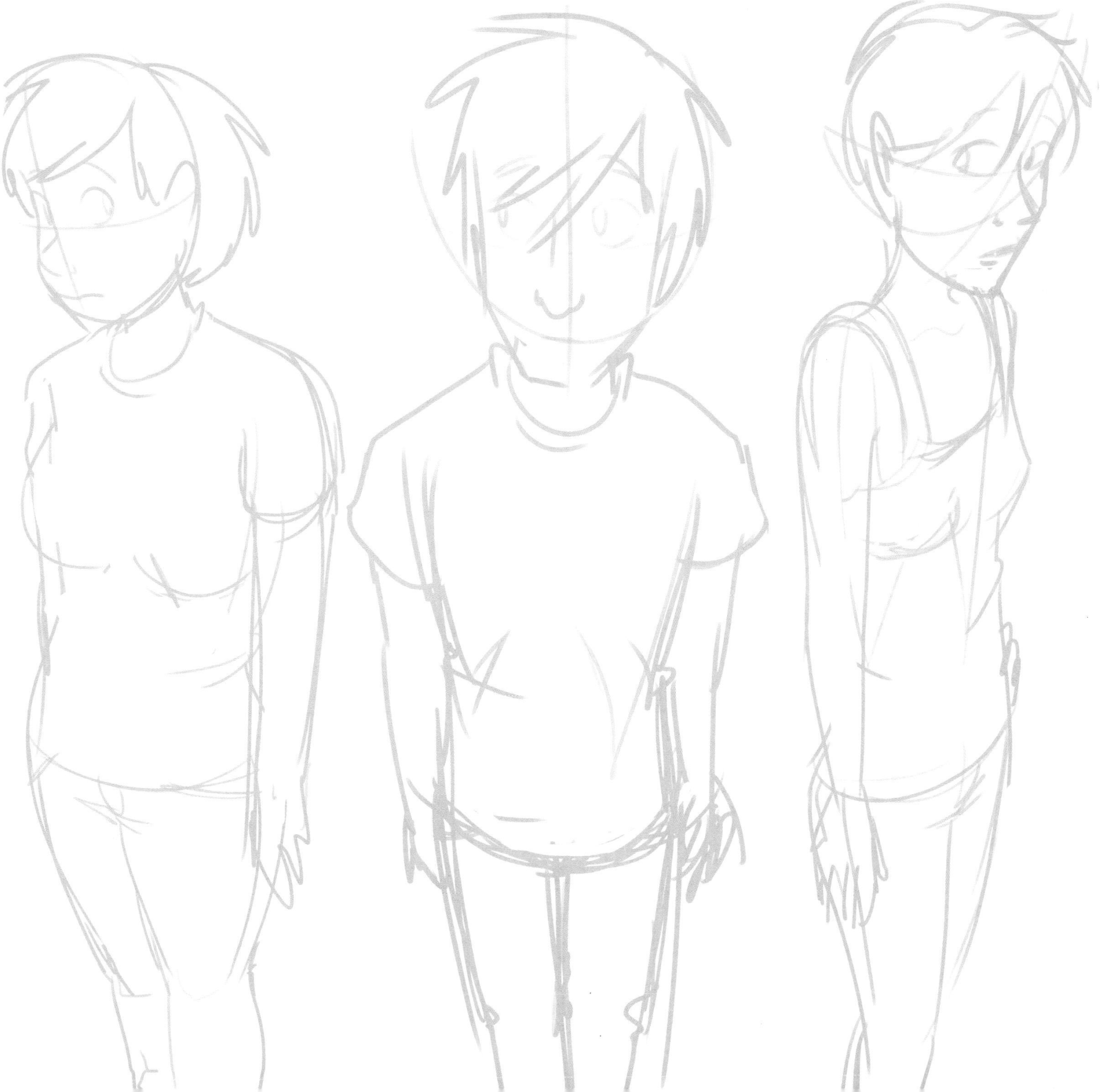

Also by Jeph Jacques:
Questionable Content Vol. 1

Published by **TopatoCo Books**, a division of **The Topato Corporation.**
116 Pleasant St. Ste 203
Easthampton, MA 01027

You can read Questionable Content for free every weekday at **questionablecontent.net!**
TopatoCo is online at **topatoco.com.**

10 9 8 7 6 5 4 3 2 1

Printed in the United States of America

First Edition, September 2011
ISBN-13: 978-1-936561-96-4

Questionable Content Vol. 2

BY JEPH JACQUES

 **TOPATOCO BOOKS** *Easthampton, Massachusetts*

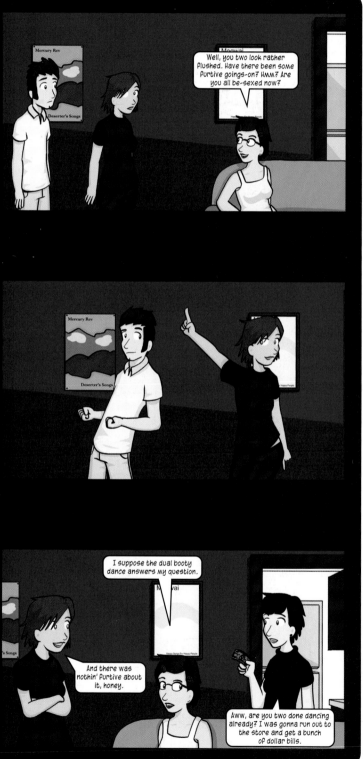

"All be-sexed" is a pretty good phrase, I think. I should use it more.

UNDERAGE DRINKING OH GOODNESS GRACIOUS

Pants from Jerkcity (that poster in the background) is one of my favorite comic characters of all time.

Number 303: Marlboro Man

how does a robot get laid, also how does a robot smoke

Number 304: I Am Bad At Connect Four

Boy, writing out Pig Latin is a lot more awkward than speaking it.

The Marten train to Dora town has since been shut down due to safety concerns.

Man, I just went CRAZY with the run-on similes back then, didn't I.

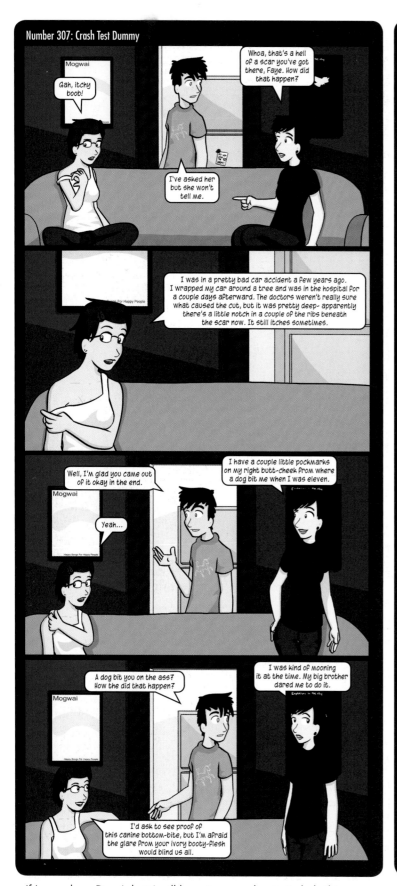

If I ever draw Dora's butt I will have to remember to include this scar.

The big Keyser Soze reveal at the end of QC will be that they totally WERE banging in the kitchen earlier.

That "hand behind the head" thing in panel 3 has kind of become Marten's signature pose. I...I guess he has a really itchy scalp?

I still get requests for duct-taped Pintsize sketches at conventions. I guess you could say that panel really...STUCK AROUND B)

Number 311: Sneaky Junk

Gah! Dammit!

What's the matter?

These stupid boxer shorts don't have a button on the front and my junk keeps sneaking out.

Fresh Cuts   *anda House*

adjust adjust

Thank you for the unnecessary briefing on the status of your boy-parts. Would you like your beating now, or when we get home later?

This from the girl who routinely grosses me out with details about her period.

The menstrual cycle is a perfectly natural part of the female reproductive system.

I didn't say it wasn't natural. I said talking about it is gross.

When you became my friend you were automatically enrolled in the Menstrual Discussion Plan. For an additional $15.99 per month you can upgrade to the Digestive Issues Bulletin Package.

Marten runs into boxer-shorts related trouble later on in the comic as well. Dude, get some better boxers!

Number 312: Solicitors Will Be Shot

Hello, are you Faye?

No Solicitors

I am indeed!

I'm Lorena Torres, we spoke on the phone about the apartment. Come on up and I'll give you a tour.

So are you new roommates?

Oh no, we've lived together for a while now. I just decided I wanted my own bedroom so I could actually get some sleep.

Oh, I...see...

You know, I think that sounded a lot more awkward out loud than it did in my head.

Don't worry about it honey, it'll take more than a little faux pas to faze me. The last couple who looked at this place was askin' if the ceiling joists were strong enough to support a sex swing.

Okay, now imagine that every single thing you say feels like that. Now you know what it is like to be me.

Always ask your realtor whether the ceiling joists are strong enough to support a sex swing.

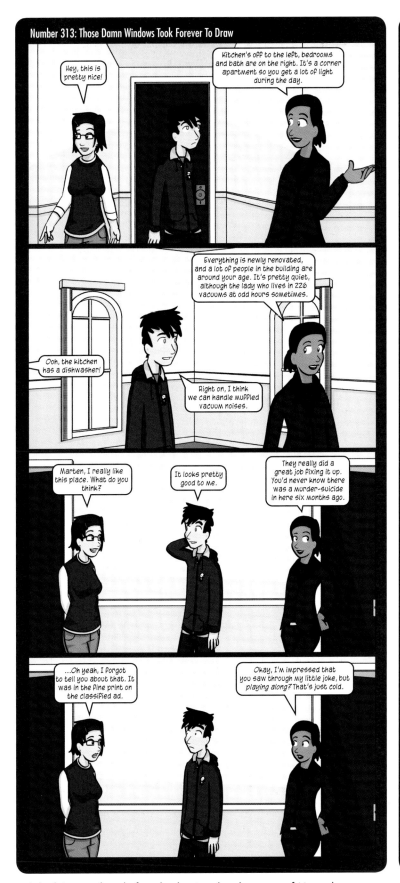

Number 313: Those Damn Windows Took Forever To Draw

I think I was already foreshadowing the character of Hannelore here in panel three, but I can't remember for sure.

Number 314: Pi

BEAT PANELS ARE THE SECRET TO COMEDY

Number 315: Altruism Is Forever

Ugh some dudes really do think the way that Marten was joking about in the last panel :\

Number 316: Post-Funny

QC VOLUME 2 DRINKING GAME: every time the punchline is a convoluted simile, take a shot.

Thirty-twelve = 360. That is a LOT of facial piercings.

Rhombuses (rhombi?) always bothered me as a kid because they were messed up squares. (also, take a shot)

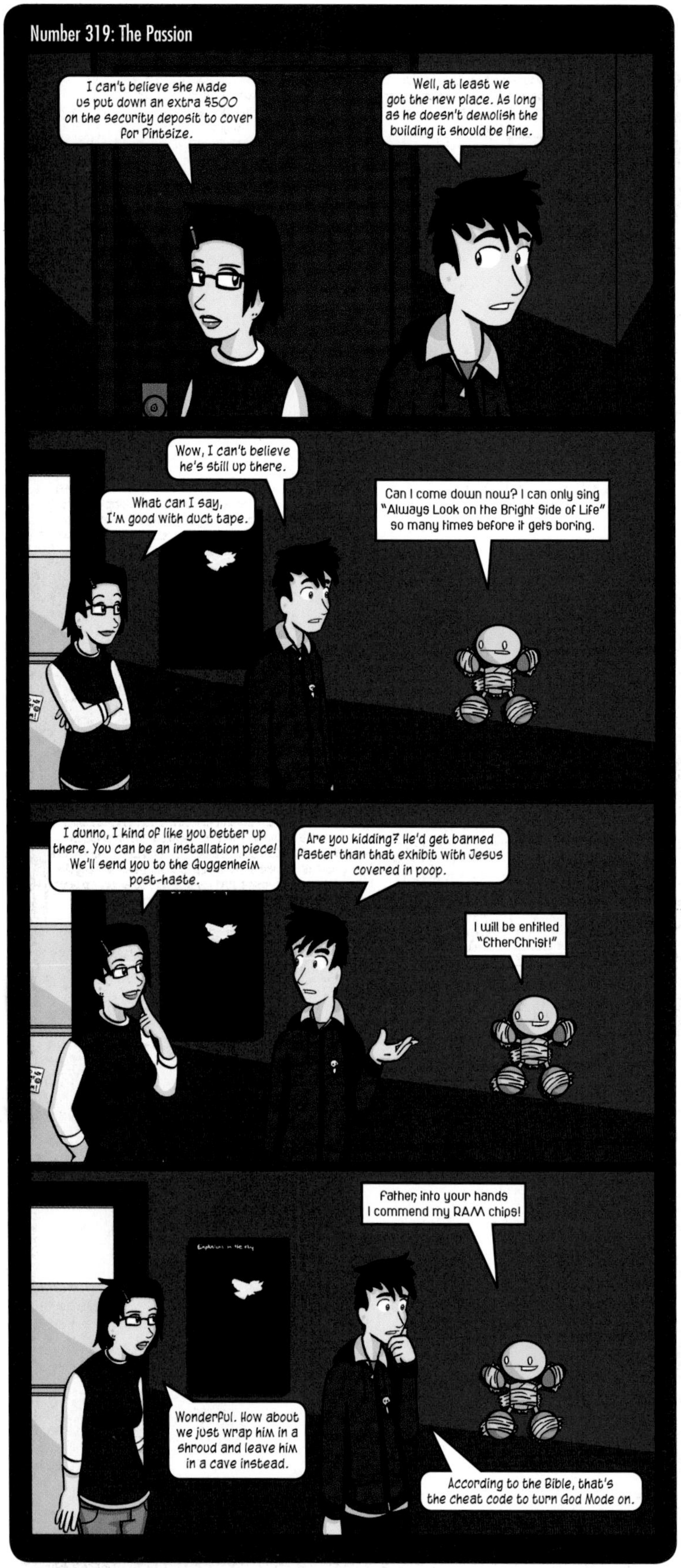
Number 319: The Passion
I can't believe she made us put down an extra $500 on the security deposit to cover for Pintsize.
Well, at least we got the new place. As long as he doesn't demolish the building it should be fine.
Wow, I can't believe he's still up there.
What can I say, I'm good with duct tape.
Can I come down now? I can only sing "Always Look on the Bright Side of Life" so many times before it gets boring.
I dunno, I kind of like you better up there. You can be an installation piece! We'll send you to the Guggenheim post-haste.
Are you kidding? He'd get banned faster than that exhibit with Jesus covered in poop.
I will be entitled "EtherChrist!"
Father, into your hands I commend my RAM chips!
Wonderful. How about we just wrap him in a shroud and leave him in a cave instead.
According to the Bible, that's the cheat code to turn God Mode on.

#punchlinesIforgotaboutthatmademelaugh
#Twitterhashtagsinprintedmaterials

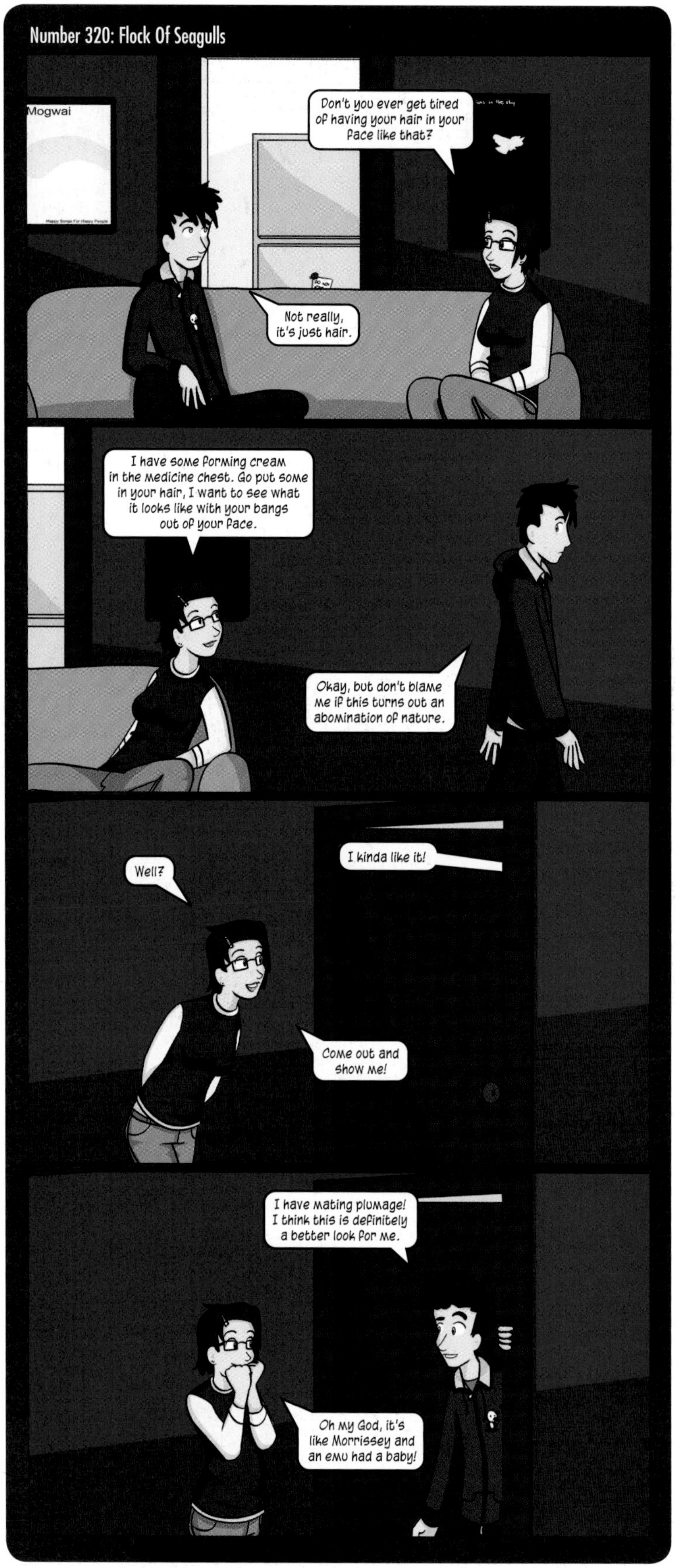
Number 320: Flock Of Seagulls
Mogwai
Don't you ever get tired of having your hair in your face like that?
Not really, it's just hair.
I have some forming cream in the medicine chest. Go put some in your hair, I want to see what it looks like with your bangs out of your face.
Okay, but don't blame me if this turns out an abomination of nature.
Well?
I kinda like it!
Come out and show me!
I have mating plumage! I think this is definitely a better look for me.
Oh my God, it's like Morrissey and an emo had a baby!

I kind of had that hair for a while when I was younger. (take a shot)

One time I was at a show at the Middle East in Boston and the two most beautiful people I had ever seen spent the entire time making out in front of me. I can't even remember the band that was playing.

It's pretty crazy how influential Pitchfork has become in the years since I wrote this comic. They're the Rolling Stone of the new millennium.

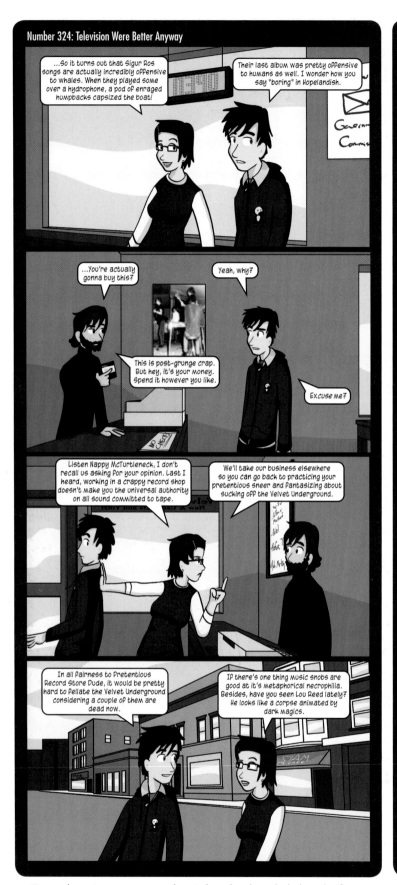

iTunes doesn't sneer at me when I download a whole bunch of Phil Collins songs.

Wow, the drawings on the chalkboard are actually a lot cuter than my "actual" art style was at this point. :\

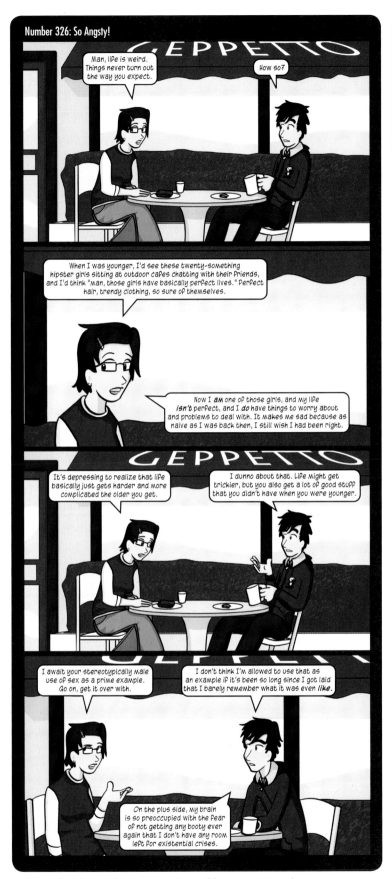

It gets harder and more complicated but sometimes there are parties!

Still pretty sure I'm right about NASCAR

Number 328: He's Quite Tall

Hi, can I help you?

Yeah, is Dora here?

Well well, if it isn't my dear older brother. You know, I was just telling some friends last night about the time you dared me to moon Mrs. Goldstein's chihuahua.

I never expected him to actually bite you, much less hang on the way he did. Tenacious little bastard.

So what brings you to my little shop? You hate coffee, I know that's not your motive.

I dunno, just thought I'd drop by and say hello. I haven't talked to you in a while. So how have you been, sis?

My life is a maelstrom of conflict, drama, and confusion.

So same old, same old. Gotcha.

Omigod your brother is totally hot! Can you set me up with him?

Sure, and while I'm at it I'll break his kneecaps and give him a case of the avian flu. It'll be a hat-trick of sibling cruelty.

What's this about hat tricks and cruelty? Are you finally starting that sado-masochistic hockey league you've always wanted?

Take a shot!

Number 329: Italo-Viking Alliance

Christ, I can't get away from this place even on my day off. Curse my caffeine addiction.

I wonder who the tall dude talking to Dora is.

Hey scarecrow, who's the beanpole?

Oh hey kids. Marten, Faye, meet my older brother Sven.

Howdy.

Wait, Sven? Sven Bianchi?

Well, mom's Swedish and dad's Italian, so...

Dad actually wanted to name me Joseph, but mom claimed naming rights since she was the one who had to give birth to me.

So is everyone in your family rail-thin like you two? What do you have for Thanksgiving dinner, two peas and a slice of turkey breast?

Yeah right. He ate half the damn turkey before I could even finish my salad last year.

It's been suggested that I'm powered by a small black hole.

Hey, at least you could use that to pick up hot lady physicists.

Do those exist?

I have met SEVERAL hot lady physicists since I wrote this comic.

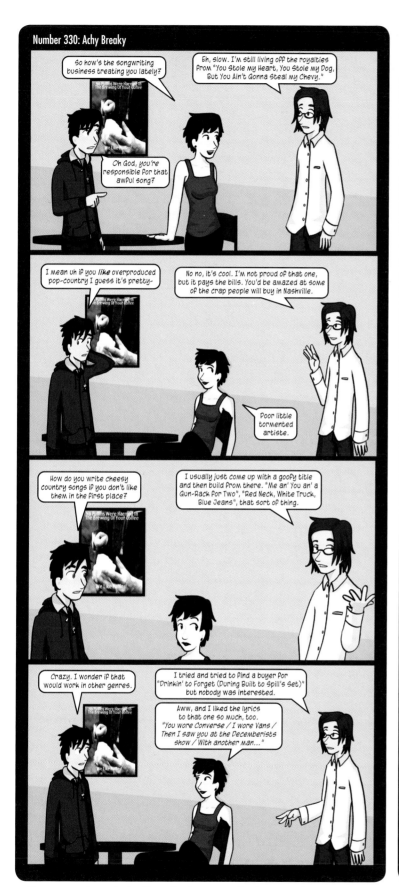

Pretty sure those lyrics Dora is singing in the last panel are an actual Death Cab For Cutie song

Take a shot. Good lord this is a dangerous drinking game.

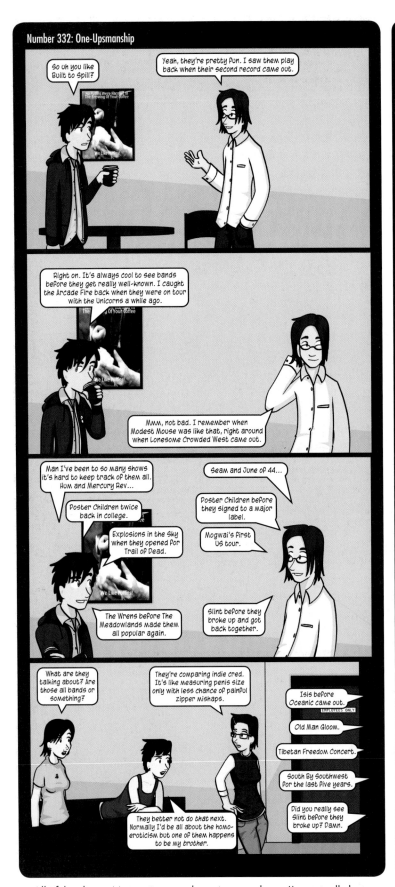

All of the shows Marten is namedropping are shows I've actually been to. (Although I didn't see the Wrens until after The Meadowlands)

Coffee of Doom: ??? Days Without A Customer Fatality

That'd be like putting a chihuahua between yourself and an angry grizzly bear.

Questionable Content does not advocate stabbing anybody in the tits.

Hahaha, seriously lollin' at Raven's line in panel four.

What kind of high school teaches anatomy? Sven that was not a very good innuendo.

Aw, I had forgotten what a sweetheart Raven was back then :3

Geez, way to blow it Pintsize

I bet there's a metalcore band out there called Your Honesty Is The Knife Twisting In The Wound That Is My Conscience.

Oh god what is up with the perspective in panel one OH GOD WHAT IS UP WITH FAYE'S FOREHEAD IN PANEL ONE D:

Seriously, I was having a huge problem with drawing characters' heads skewed way forward and never even realized it, aaaaugh.

Faye's FAQ is 3.2 MB and extremely convoluted.

Nietzsche-Os: What's he Point™

God damn Faye that is just ROUGH of you.

Number 346: It Would Be Pretty Cute

Oh god that IS pretty adorable

Number 347: Don't Be A Robo-Homophobe

Silly Faye, gender is much, much more complicated than that.

Number 348: Like A John Cusack Movie

I don't know what a destroyosaur looks like but it can't be good.

Number 349: If He's Busy, Call Slash

I can hum the guitar solo for "November Rain" by Guns 'N Roses in its entirety. It was a weird day when I discovered this.

If there were save points for ladies, people would just constantly replay the high school level over and over.

Damn that's a short skirt!

Somehow Marten's line in panel three ended up on a lot of those "famous people quotes" internet pages.

Man whatever Faye curvy girls fukken rule

Number 354: Purple Hearts

The 1970s were not a great time for clothing.

Number 355: What About The Bananas?

I like to think the waitress had been standing behind them the entire time, just WAITING to chime in with a witty quip.

Dolphins are pretty much always down to fuck

Cute Goth Boy In The Corner, a new fragrance by Questionable Content

Would unironically listen to that song

I dunno, gouda smells pretty good most of the time.

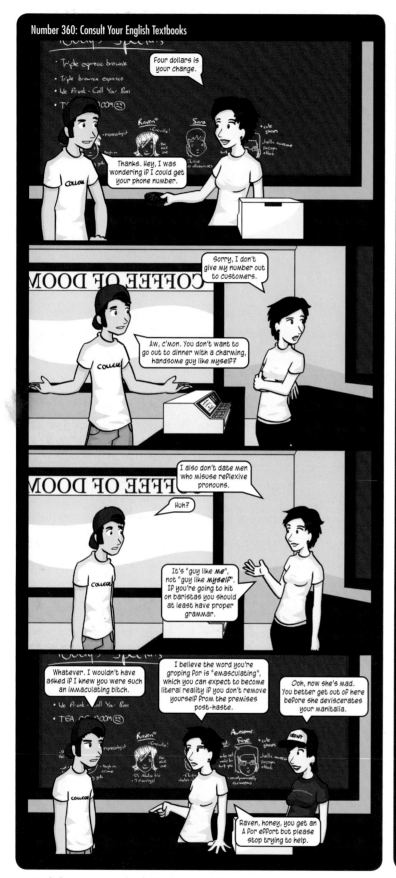

God damn, Raven had ALL the good lines back then.

Crazy street musicians are a staple of Northampton culture.

taaaake a shooooot

Faye those are not mutant powers that is a panic attack

Minutes later, both Dora and Raven were being treated for severe concussion.

You should probably stop taking shots, we're not even 1/3 of the way through this book.

Number 366: Stay Out Of The Pit

Ooh, here comes the waiter.

Hey, he looks kinda familiar.

Afternoon everybody, can I get you some drinks before you order?

Excuse me, but were you at the Converge show two weeks ago?

Yeah, why do you...oh hey, I remember you! You were the chick who kicked me in the face during "You Fail Me"!

I knew you looked familiar! Man, that pit was crazy.

You totally knocked out one of my teeth with your boot.

Yeah, I found it on the floor after the show. I wanted to give it back but I couldn't find you in the crowd. It's on my dresser at home if you want it.

That'd be rad. Can you bring it by later on? I get off at seven tonight. My name's Amir, by the way.

I'm Nat. Sorry about kicking you in the face.

Nah, it's cool.

This is the weirdest courtship I have ever witnessed.

The scary part is that this is pretty normal for Natasha.

Converge are still around! That is crazy.

Number 367: Or Meg White, It's Up To You

So let me get this straight— you kicked this guy in the face in a mosh pit and knocked out one of his friggin' teeth, and now he asks you for your phone number?

Yeah, pretty much. What's the big deal?

I just don't get the whole hardcore "we beat the shit out of each other and then hug" thing.

She took me to a concert once but between the scary screaming and the scary kids punching each other I didn't like it much.

That's just how the scene is. Either you understand or you don't.

Well, whatever floats your boat I guess. I feel a lot safer at indie rock shows where everyone just stands there with their arms folded.

That is so lame. At a hardcore show you can break a dude's nose and he'll high-five you, but if you accidentally make eye contact with someone at an indie show it's the biggest social faux pas ever.

Indie kids are like gorillas— peaceful by nature, but if you make eye contact they see it as a challenge.

A challenge to what, see who has the biggest boner for Stephen Malkmus?

Natasha!

Actually it's usually the chick from Cat Power. She's hot.

It's weird to see Steve talking about indie rock shows, I see him as much more of a "bro" these days.

37

I can't believe it's 2011 and punk bands are still doing that.

Questionable Content: Ice Cream Is Delicious

This may be the quintessential Raven strip.

oh god that pun ugh

Oh come on Marten the implications aren't THAT staggering

Poop jokes + art references = SUCCESS

Marten and Dora look similar to this day. I've tried to differentiate them! It just doesn't work very well. :\

I think there really are people who go through life just looking for things to be angry about.

41

BLAAAAAAHDWIN

If you've ever seen Pintsize's Twitter account you know that furry porn is one of the most HARMLESS things on the internet, comparatively.

I actually don't blame Faye at all here. Don't slap your friends on the butt! It's weird!

I'm glad I got sick of "Faye threatens violence" as a punchline relatively early on.

MEN, amirite?

I like to think she still puts him in that box when he misbehaves sometimes.

or children :(

You don't actually want a pony, Faye. Ponies are kind of jerks.

45

Never put anything past Pintsize.

WILL SHE PUT THE SHORTS ON???

...yes?

The tungsten carbide of femininity is much better for the environment and has similar armor-penetrating properties.

Number 388: To Say Nothing Of The Crisco Incident

You think that's bad, try finding A STRANGER'S dirty underwear in your sink.

Number 389: Brother Faye

I should get a monk's robe. It would make writing comics feel less blasphemous.

It's not an issue of data loss, he just has a weird phobia of electromagnets.

"The horizontal demolition derby" wins the award for worst sex euphemism I have ever coined.

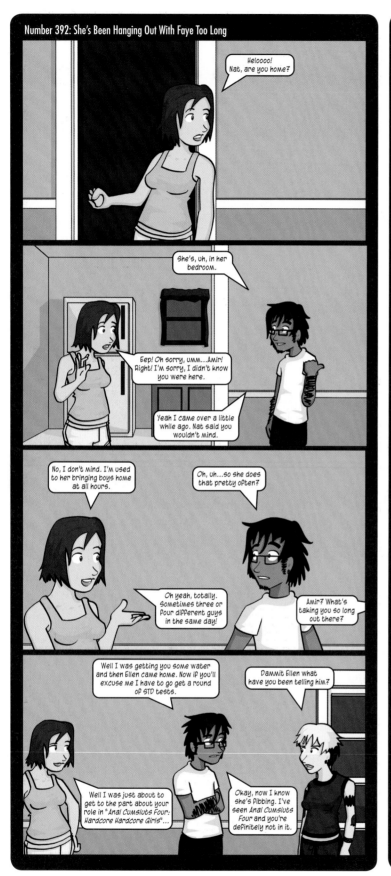

Heloooo! Nat, are you home?

She's, uh, in her bedroom.

Eep! Oh sorry, umm...Amir! Right! I'm sorry, I didn't know you were here.

Yeah I came over a little while ago. Nat said you wouldn't mind.

No, I don't mind. I'm used to her bringing boys home at all hours.

Oh, uh...so she does that pretty often?

Oh yeah, totally. Sometimes three or four different guys in the same day!

Amir? What's taking you so long out there?

Well I was getting you some water and then Ellen came home. Now if you'll excuse me I have to go get a round of STD tests.

Dammit Ellen what have you been telling him?

Well I was just about to get to the part about your role in "Anal Cumsluts Four: Hardcore Hardcore Girls"...

Okay, now I know she's fibbing. I've seen Anal Cumsluts Four and you're definitely not in it.

Anal Cumsluts Three is widely regarded as the high water mark of the series

Hey you, beer, boys, and Chinese food are here. Where's your roomie?

Nah, she's busy with her new boyfriend or whatever.

That's fine, more booze and wontons for me then. Come sit!

Wow, you guys sure got things set up fast.

Arranging furniture is easier when you're fortified with alcohol.

I'm the foreman! The couch needs to move six inches to the left to achieve maximum feng shui!

You're going to become an end table if you don't cut it out.

Oh yeah, that'd be great. Wandering off with your drink, eating your hors d'oeuvres...

Where's Steve, anyway?

He's usin' the bathroom.

You might not want to go in there for a while.

Drat, I wanted to be first to deflower our virgin lavatory.

I am not comfortable with that imagery at all.

Well, deflowering is one of Steve's few marketable skills.

I'm good at deforestation.

I like Pintsize's lil' head popping up in that last panel, just desperate to squeeze in one last quip.

Why I don't do comics about indie bands anymore, in a nutshell.

Neon Genesis JudeLawvangeion

Sheesh, Marten sure was being awfully forward at this point.

I sold Faye's "Sellout" shirt for a while. I guess you could say I… SOLD OU-[gunshots, explosions]

I don't want to spoil future plot twists for you, but Faye and Dora both die in a car crash in comic 400.

aaaaaaaugh Pizza Girl's head in panel one. This may be the most awkward period in the evolution of my art style. I'm sorry :(

Oh look they didn't die in a car crash after all!

Oh man remember VJs?

He baked them a delicious cake and taught them how to tie their shoes!

BJORN HAVE VERY BAD DAY.

Faye feels like doing that pretty much every Thursday.

Are the Hapsburgs still around?

Good lord look how giant I was drawing their heads at this point! It's…kinda cute?

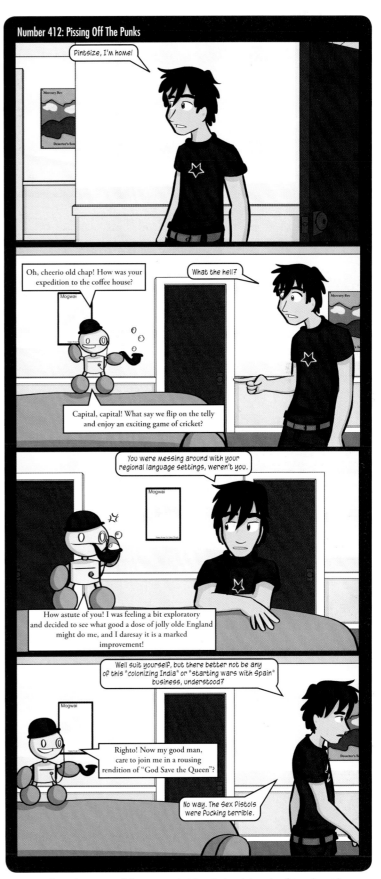

I wonder what a serif font sounds like. I should make friends with a synesthetic person and ask them.

The logical extension of the exclamation "what the hell" is "what the hell ass," followed in intensity by "what the hell ass balls."

Six years later, Marten's prediction has essentially come true. :(

Number 415: He Didn't Miss The Good Part

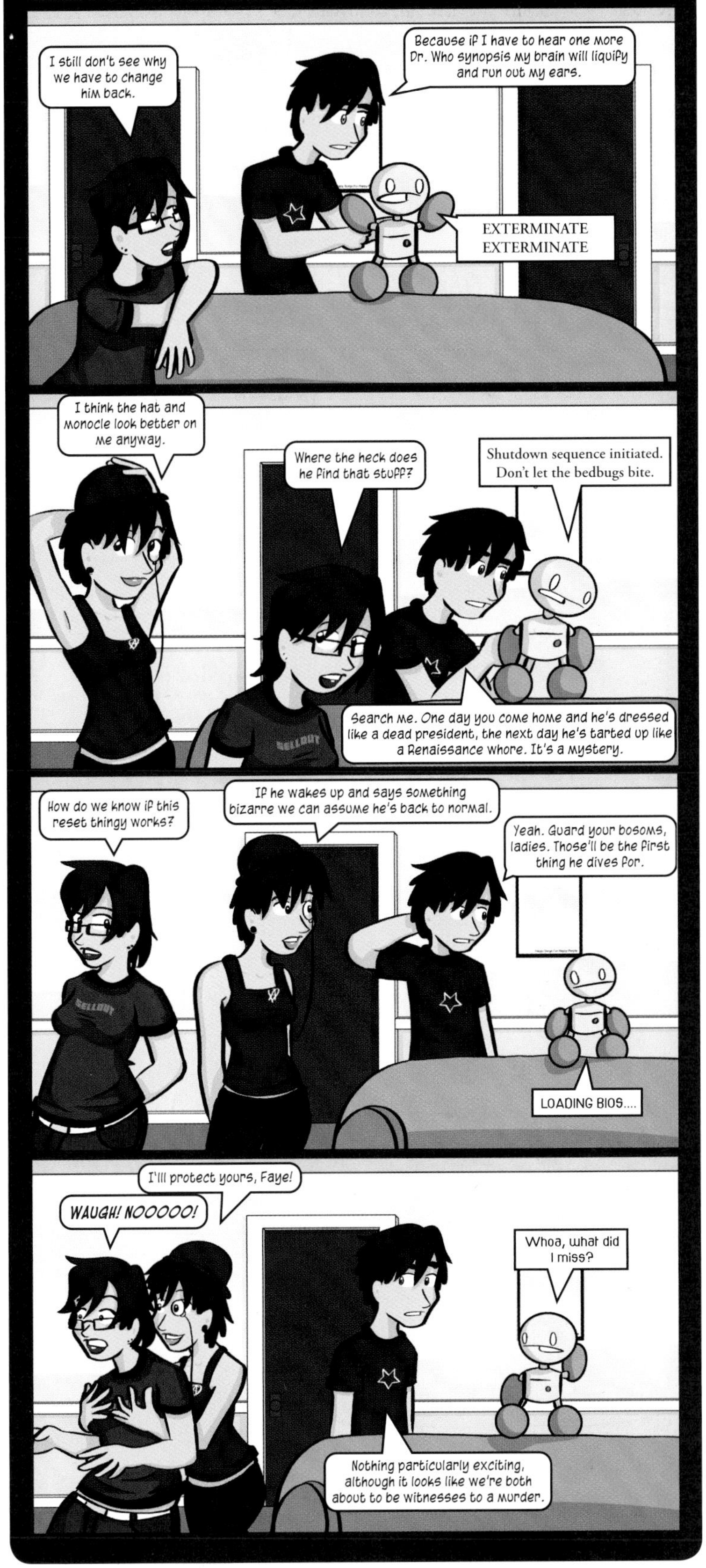

I still don't see why we have to change him back.
Because if I have to hear one more Dr. Who synopsis my brain will liquify and run out my ears.
EXTERMINATE EXTERMINATE
I think the hat and monocle look better on me anyway.
Where the heck does he find that stuff?
Shutdown sequence initiated. Don't let the bedbugs bite.
Search me. One day you come home and he's dressed like a dead president, the next day he's tarted up like a Renaissance whore. It's a mystery.
How do we know if this reset thingy works?
If he wakes up and says something bizarre we can assume he's back to normal.
Yeah. Guard your bosoms, ladies. Those'll be the first thing he dives for.
LOADING BIOS....
WAUGH! NOOOOO!
I'll protect yours, Faye!
Whoa, what did I miss?
Nothing particularly exciting, although it looks like we're both about to be witnesses to a murder.

Six years later, Dr. Who is more popular than it has ever been. Truly I am the Kwisatz Haderach.

Number 416: Don't Push Your Luck

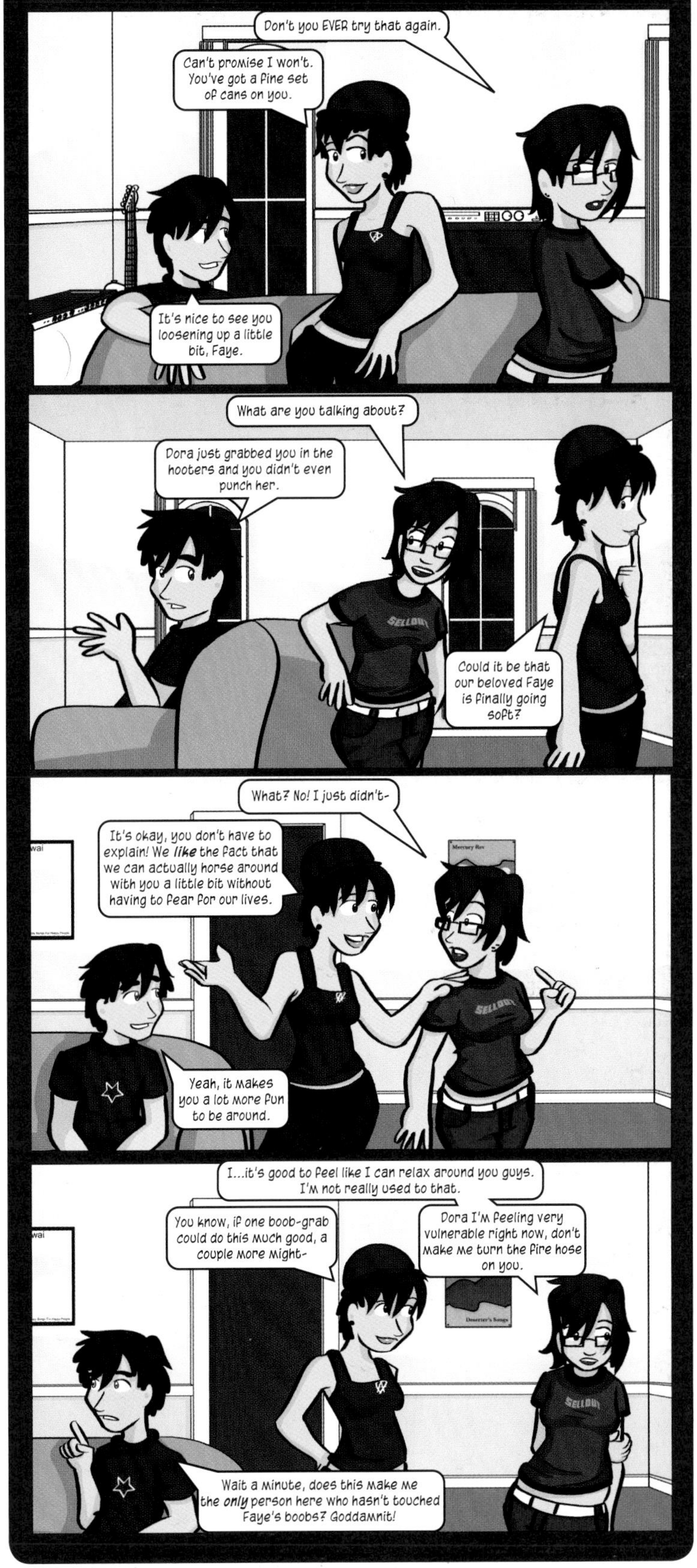

Don't you EVER try that again.
Can't promise I won't. You've got a fine set of cans on you.
It's nice to see you loosening up a little bit, Faye.
What are you talking about?
Dora just grabbed you in the hooters and you didn't even punch her.
Could it be that our beloved Faye is finally going soft?
What? No! I just didn't-
It's okay, you don't have to explain! We like the fact that we can actually horse around with you a little bit without having to fear for our lives.
Yeah, it makes you a lot more fun to be around.
I...it's good to feel like I can relax around you guys. I'm not really used to that.
You know, if one boob-grab could do this much good, a couple more might-
Dora I'm feeling very vulnerable right now, don't make me turn the fire hose on you.
Wait a minute, does this make me the only person here who hasn't touched Faye's boobs? Goddamnit!

1500 strips later as of this printing, I don't believe Marten has ever touched Faye's boobs.

Silly Pintsize, Martha Stewart doesn't HAVE blood!

GENDER STEREOTYPES

I like how Dora is still wearing Pintsize's bowler hat.

Can you tell I really like Viking metal?

That would definitely not be ethical.

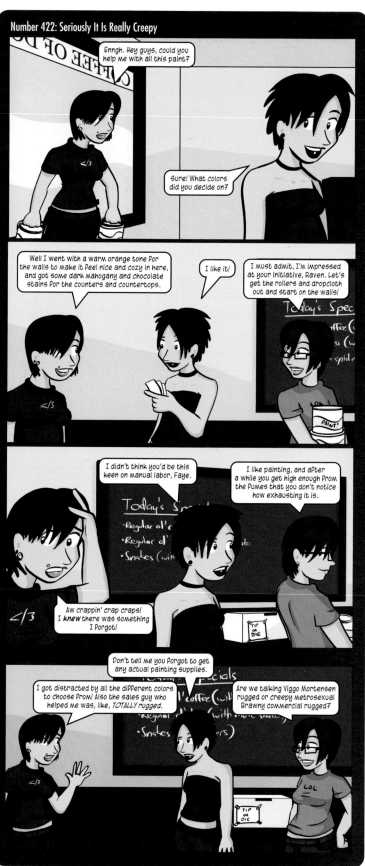

Wanna start a band called Rugged Bros

The joke is that a human being could not possibly survive the G-forces generated by that kind of acceleration

"Cognitive slagheap." DAAAAAAANG

I think this was the comic where I finally had to go and look up the word "hirsute" to make sure I wasn't using it incorrectly.

I like that hallucinatey effect in the last panel. I should use that more.

The joke is that Faye is drinking pure sodium chloride (the second joke is that there is no reason for AnthroPCs to be drinking it either)

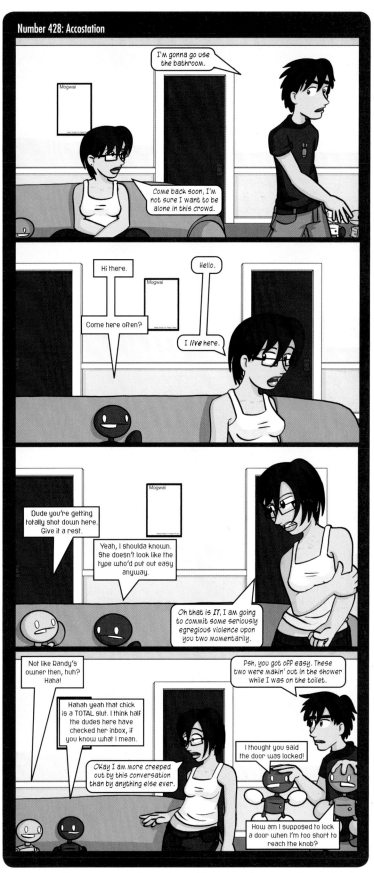

Robot make-outs are really awkward because their mouths just kind of bonk into each other.

Oof, I was trying for a kind of 4/5-perspective on Marten's face in this one but really didn't know how to do it yet. THE JOYS OF LEARNING TO DRAW IN PUBLIC ON THE INTERNET.

Okay it's a little better in this one.

Say hello to Marten's mom! One of the most popular supporting characters in the entire series. I have a lot of fun with her.

Richie Wilson was still never seen alive again.

Number 433: Ye Olde Backstorey

So, you must be the infamous Faye! Marty's told me all about you.

Oh uh hopefully he left out the bad stuff at least. Nice to meet you, Mrs. Reed.

I prefer *Miss* Reed, actually. Seeing as I'm not married anymore and all.

Oh, I'm sorry! I didn't think about that.

No offense taken.

How come you never told me your parents were divorced?

I dunno, it never really came up in conversation.

Marty doesn't like to talk about it. It was a difficult time. Imagine being a ten year old boy and discovering that not only are your mother and father getting a divorce, but your father has just come out of the closet about his homosexuality.

Well the gay thing wasn't really much of a shock.

Why not? It was certainly news to me at the time.

Did *you* ever rummage through dad's sock drawer? "Marine Man-Wich Volumes 1 Through 4" was a pretty big tipoff.

You know, I always wondered why he insisted on folding and arranging his socks himself.

Marine Man-Wich 5: Return To Volleyball Cove

Number 434: Ice Ice Baby

Do you keep in contact with your dad at all now?

Oh yeah, of course.

Henry and I are still friends. he actually has a nightclub down in Miami now.

I suppose it was really more a marriage of convenience anyway. Henry and I were lonely, and we both wanted a family. We got along well so it seemed like the right thing to do, but I think we make better friends and parents than husband and wife.

Henry's been seeing a wonderful fellow named Marcel for the last few years. They make a better couple than he and I ever did.

While you, meanwhile, run around dating guys half your age.

Dating? Oh heavens no! I just have lots and lots of casual sex. It's all the fun of dating without any of the fuss.

Mom I know I'm an adult now and all but there are really limits to how candid you should be with your children.

Oh hush, just because you aren't getting any tail doesn't mean I can't talk about it.

Man, that is colder than a penguin's third nipple. I like your mom, Marty.

The joke is that penguins are not mammals and therefore do not possess nipples

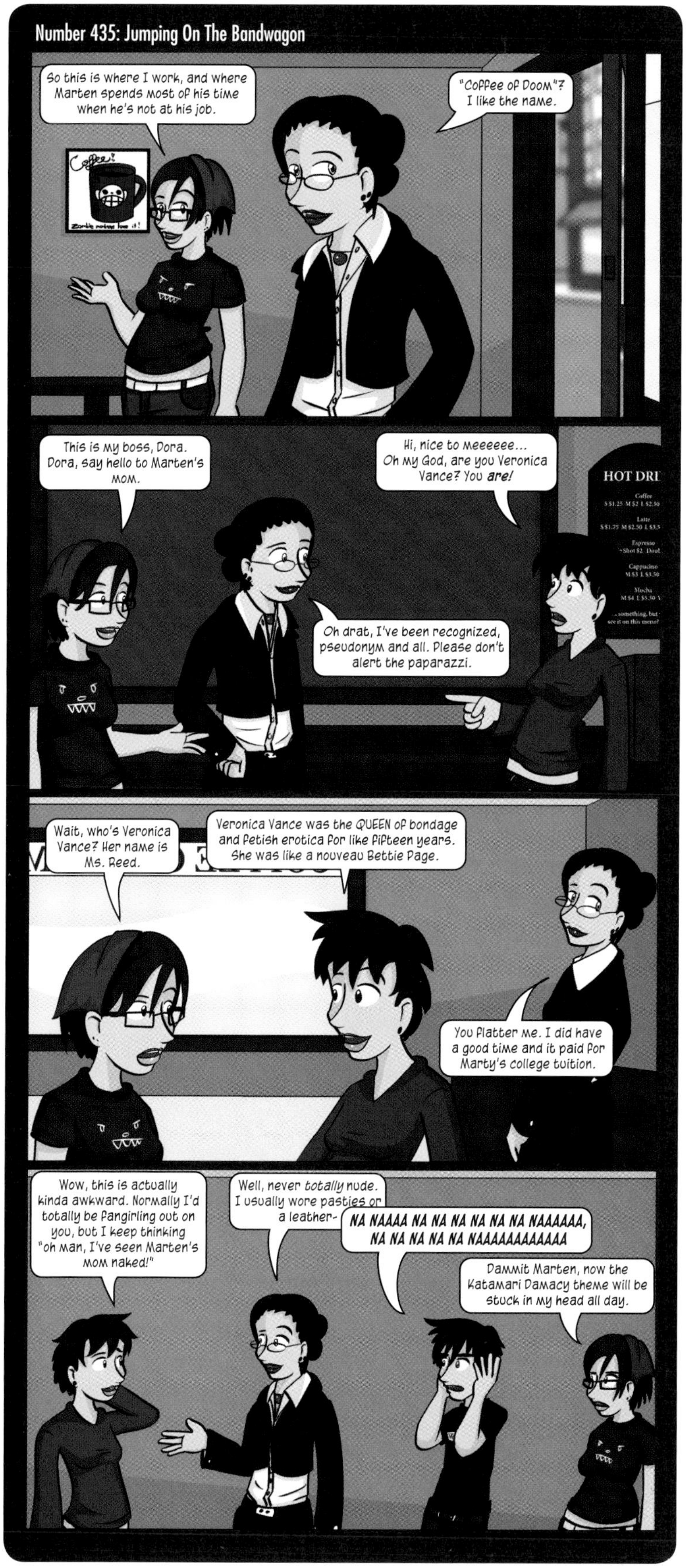
Number 435: Jumping On The Bandwagon
So this is where I work, and where Marten spends most of his time when he's not at his job.
"Coffee of Doom"? I like the name.
This is my boss, Dora. Dora, say hello to Marten's mom.
Hi, nice to meeeeee... Oh my God, are you Veronica Vance? You are!
Oh drat, I've been recognized, pseudonym and all. Please don't alert the paparazzi.
HOT DRI
Wait, who's Veronica Vance? Her name is Ms. Reed.
Veronica Vance was the QUEEN of bondage and fetish erotica for like fifteen years. She was like a nouveau Bettie Page.
You flatter me. I did have a good time and it paid for Marty's college tuition.
Wow, this is actually kinda awkward. Normally I'd totally be fangirling out on you, but I keep thinking "oh man, I've seen Marten's mom naked!"
Well, never totally nude. I usually wore pasties or a leather-
NA NAAAA NA NA NA NA NA NA NAAAAAA, NA NA NA NA NA NAAAAAAAAAAA
Dammit Marten, now the Katamari Damacy theme will be stuck in my head all day.

I can STILL feel the friggin' cosmos.

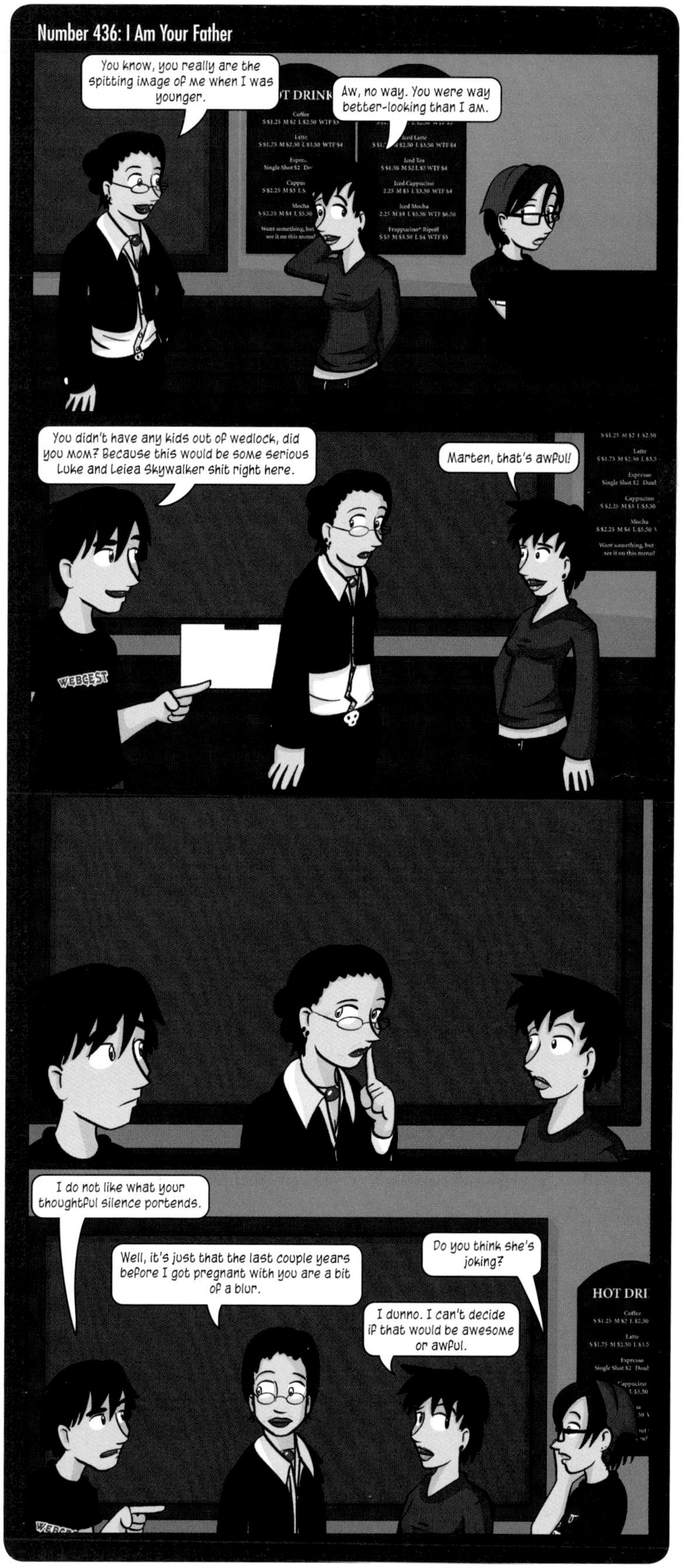
Number 436: I Am Your Father
You know, you really are the spitting image of me when I was younger.
Aw, no way. You were way better-looking than I am.
You didn't have any kids out of wedlock, did you mom? Because this would be some serious Luke and Leiea Skywalker shit right here.
Marten, that's awful!
WEBCEST
I do not like what your thoughtful silence portends.
Well, it's just that the last couple years before I got pregnant with you are a bit of a blur.
Do you think she's joking?
I dunno. I can't decide if that would be awesome or awful.
HOT DRI

This will not be the last time their resemblance is remarked upon.

You know, Marten, if you would just stick WITH the flirty comments and not immediately backtrack into awkwardness, you might get somewhere with a lady eventually.

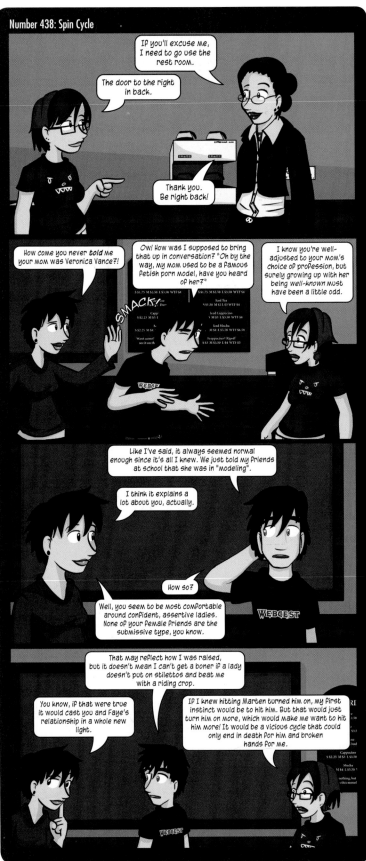

Growing up knowing I was adopted (PS I'm adopted) was like what Marten is talking about- everyone ELSE found it a lot more unusual than I ever did.

Still no female robots in love with Marten, 1500 strips later.

Science has not found any evidence of a delicious chocolate core, but proponents of nougatgenesis remain optimistic.

Number 441: Tee, Tee Em Eye

So there I am, covered in peanut oil and brandishing a large trout, when his *cell phone* goes off.

Oh man, talk about bad timing.

Aw man, that's horrible.

Actually it was great timing. It was set to vibrate mode, so his prostate got a nice little massage.

What can I say, Marty? Your father and I had some adventurous times together.

What?! That was *DAD* you were talking about?! Jesus shit!

Oh, I'm just pulling your leg. It wasn't really Henry.

Sheesh, thank God. I mean, it's one thing if you're doing weird stuff with one of your clients, but that was just a little bit too close to home for comfort.

Actually, I was just kidding *then.* It really was your father.

Augh! Nooo!

This really puts the time I caught my parents in the missionary position in a broader perspective.

The weird part was that Dora's parents were just doing their taxes!

Number 442: Wallet Photo

So are you originally from this area?

Yep. My parents spend most of their time in Florida now, but my big brother and I still live here in town.

And you run Coffee of Doom yourself?

Uh huh. It consistently fails to drive me into bankruptcy so I must be doing something right.

Hah, spoken like a true entrepreneur.

Do you have a boyfriend?

Nah, my cat would freak out. He gets very jealous of other men.

He seemed to like me just fine... wait, does that mean I've been emasculated by a *cat?* Dammit!

It's okay, Marten. He was emasculated by the vet in a much more literal sense, which is a lot worse.

I dunno, at least he got anaesthetic for that.

Aw man check out that SWEET leaf pattern-stamp! Vintage Adobe Photoshop action in dis comic.

72

Imagine the advances he would have made in electrician-science!

Man, I get what I was going for with the art at this point, but Faye just doesn't look like Faye without the little button nose she normally has.

Number 445: Like Two Angry Ferrets

This could still happen at any moment.

Number 446: How To Make Mom Happy

What IS the opposite of a punch? A hug? A handshake? Those both seem like things you could do in front of someone's mom.

Number 447: Alternative Lifestyles

Pintsize just fell into his big prop box and came out looking like that.

Number 448: Nslookup

THINLY VEILED REFERENCES TO MY OWN LIFE AT THAT TIME COMICS

The next day Marten found a live trout flopping around on Pintsize's hard drive. #heyooo

Wombats have teeth like chisels, man. I would not want a wombat to the face.

QC Writing Tip #105: "When pressed for ideas, set a character's butt on fire."

I read this comic and thought "wow, Faye likes some surprisingly mainstream indie-rock bands." HIPSTER TRAP SPRUNG...ON MYSELF

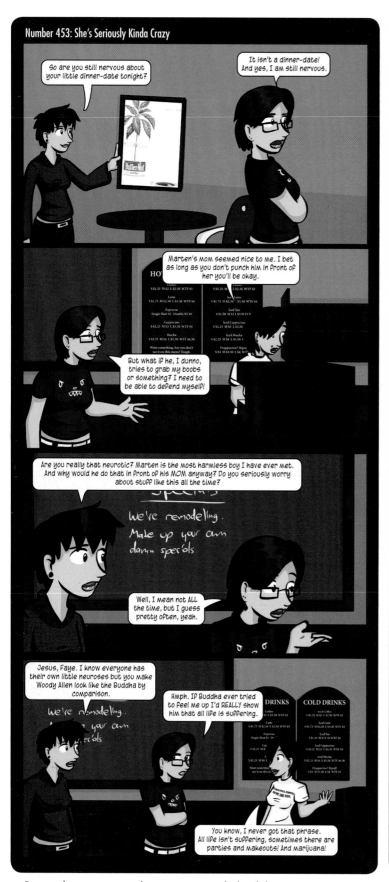

Raven does not grasp the core concept behind that quote. OR DOES SHE???

The curtain is beginning to be lifted on Faye's issues. You'll find out exactly what the big secret is…IN THIS VERY BOOK! :o

Number 455: Final Wishes

Pissfiddle (noun): A fiddle filled partially with liquid (traditionally horse-urine) to create a particular sound quality. Commonly paired with the poopdrum and vomitharp in ensembles.

Number 456: See, They Get Along

Delicious delicious animal muscle

Then Marten learned to check for visible Adam's-apples and his life changed forever.

And she did it SIMULTANEOUSLY.

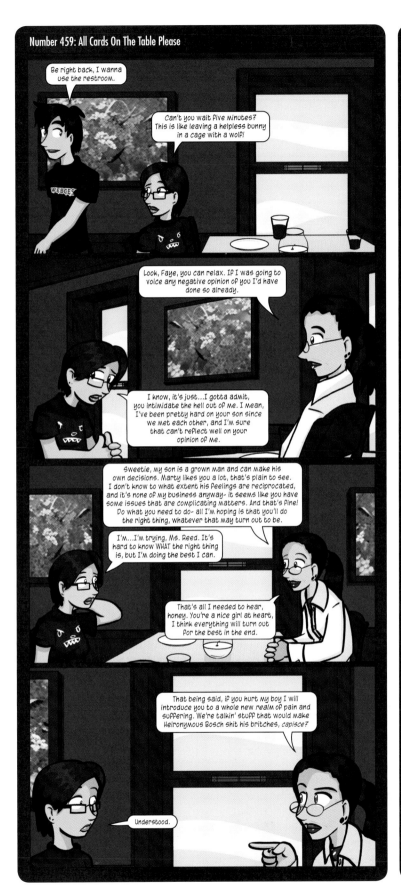

I'm pretty sure there are more words just in panel 3 than in an entire comic I write, these days. I've really cut down the dialog.

Marten's grandpa is just getting laid CONSTANTLY

I will never, ever stop making Dune jokes, this I swear.

The judge has some problems at home, he dreads the end of each workday. His life is a sad one.

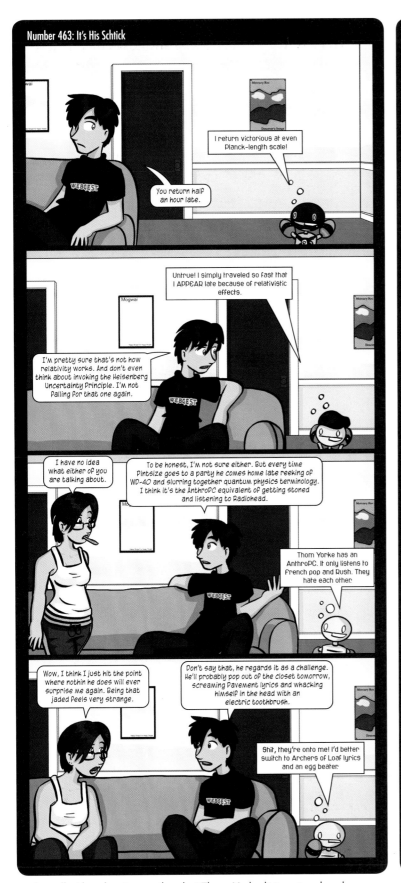

Actually I bet that is exactly what Thom Yorke listens to when he is by himself.

You'd think the milk would leak out of the disc-drive slot or something.

That blog is still up, actually! It just hasn't been updated in years.

Talk to your robo-doctor about robo-incontinence today.

And Raven comes in out of left-field with the non-sequitir punchline!

She could just use the pommel, Dora.

Number 469: Then You Ride A Unicycle

This was one of those strips where I had no idea if it would be funny to anyone other than me. Turns out those are frequently the most popular comics!

Number 470: Possibly Justified

She had an emergency, OKAY?

"To be honest, I always figured she'd snap and do something like this eventually."

Steve looks more or less how I do every time I wake up, hungover or not. I am not a morning person.

That is, ironically, how I ended up proposing to my wife.

It's the Tequila Monster! Tequila Monster ALWAYS thinks you should drink more.

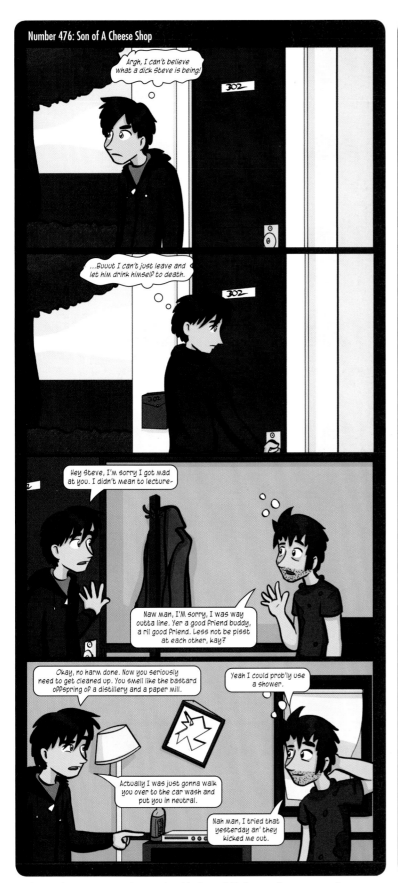

Steve then attempted to order McDonald's by walking up to the drive-through window.

Li'l Stevie Ray Vaughn has some sick riffs, dude.

Faye's line in panel four is another one that people quote a lot.

Hahahaha that is a sick burn on the Killers in panel 4

Faye was gonna back-rub her to death.

AS A HAPPILY MARRIED MAN I HEREBY DENOUNCE THE PUNCHLINE OF THIS COMIC, MARRIED LIFE IS WONDERFUL (please send help) (just kidding)

HIPSTER METAL

A while back I did the math, and Dora and Faye would have to be working 60-80 hour weeks unless there were a whole bunch of other employees we never see. So much for the suspension of your disbelief!

One know, I've had a dog for over a year now, and she's never chewed up any of MY stilettos.

One time I fired up a drum machine app on my iPhone and then ran it through a guitar amp, it sounded AMAZING

Fun fact: I used to live on Ward Ave. in Easthampton! NOT ANYMORE THOUGH, SORRY STALKERS

I have met readers who were Suicide Girls. It's a little odd to be talking to someone in person and thinking "I've seen you naked on the internet."

I don't think art school would have helped Hitler much.

At least he tries, though!

Being a robot, Pintsize is an extremely objective judge of breast quality.

The third testicle is on his back D:

Number 492: As Seen In Jackie Chan Movies

You know, it's nice to see that you're able to joke around about some of your issues, Faye.

Well, I'm trying to be a little better about dealing with things. Humor is a good way of maintaining control and distance over otherwise traumatic stuff.

Oh, totally. That's why when I die I want my corpse to be packed with gunpowder and catapulted into a Hawaiian volcano. No mourning allowed!

Hah! Will you be wearing a lei and a floral shirt?

Yep. Nude from the waist down.

What's this about nudity?

You missed it, we all got naked at my apartment and danced around like monkeys.

Suuure. And my cat wears a monocle and drinks cognac.

I'm pretty sure kitties aren't supposed to drink alcohol.

Cats no, Faye yes! Drinky drinky!

I call dibs on any and all nude monkey dancing.

Christ, you've barely cracked open the bottle and already your sentence structure is down the tubes. This'll be a fun night.

If you give a monkey alcohol it will become an unstoppable martial artist!

I like Marten's funeral idea a lot, actually.

Number 493: Ambushed!

I bet at the end of the movie he ends up matin' with the Queen Raptor.

I'm sure that would please the Sci-Fi Channel's undoubtedly large furry demographic.

Run, Lorenzo Lamas! Run from the dinosaurs!

No no, that's zoophilia. It'd be furry porn if he were DRESSED UP as a raptor and bangin' a chick in an iguana costume.

Gotta pee gotta pee

"Next on Sci-Fi- Raptor Island 2: Furry Island! A land where the law of the jungle is yipp or be yipped!"

Run, Lorenzo Lamas! Run from the furries!

Meow!

EEEK!

BONK!

THUD

Dude I think your cat just bludgeoned Raven to death.

Man, I hope not. I can see myself now, testifyin' against him in court, dual coverage by CNN and Animal Planet, PETA protestin' outside the courthouse...

When a housecat kills a human he is regarded as a god by his feline peers.

They'd kill us all if they could.

Baby won't you kiss / kiss on my bump / smooch on that lump / baby baby kiss on my bump

The only hard one to get would be Faye.

Number 496: Like A Log

Much as I hate to deny Marten any more opportunities for sexual harassment, it's time I went home and got some sleep.

Aww, you're not even fall-down drunk yet! Where's the fun in that?

Hey, I'm glad she's not totally smashed. Means my junk won't be.

I'd ask if I'll ever live that headbutting incident down, but I've never been a fan of needless rhetoric.

Honey if you think your junk is EVER safe around her you're sorely mistaken.

Thank you for the lovely evening, Dora. We'll have to return the favor sometime.

No worries. It was good to have some other humans in the apartment for once. Helps keep the voices quiet, you know?

I'm going to assume you were either joking or referring to some noisy neighbors.

What are you going to do about Raven?

Oh, I'll let her sleep. I'll just take her pants and hold them hostage tomorrow morning until she agrees to buy me breakfast.

You might want to rinse her hair off in the sink while you're at it, before her hair gel permanently fuses her to the upholstery.

zzzzzzzzz

It's extremely powerful hair gel.

Number 497: Flights Of Fancy

I had fun tonight!

I'm sure you did. It's not every night you get your bottom randomly grabbed by a lady.

Oh come on, you gotta admit it was pretty funny.

Raven does have a knack for putting me in my place, I suppose.

I'm just glad she didn't try to kiss you or anything. Bleah.

Yeah, that would have been bad.

It would have been even worse if she had gotten topless and climbed up on my

OKAY YES THAT WOULD BE BAD NOW MAY WE DISEMBARK FROM THIS TRAIN OF THOUGHT PLEASE

TERRIBLE, TERRIBLE THOUGHTS

TURKEYS

Wait, didn't I do that "aging indie bands turn into hippies" gag earlier? SHIT.

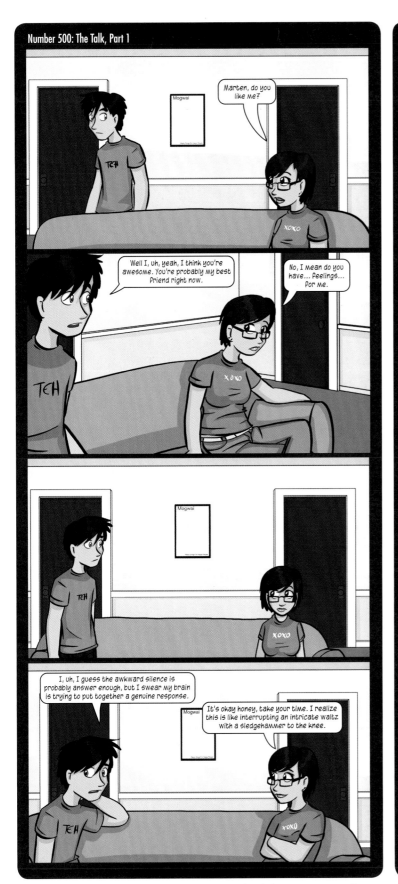

The beginning of what would come to be the defining moment of the comic. Still can't believe where it went from here.

Yes Marten, you have been so subtle about it all this time, it is AMAZING that Faye figured out you were into her.

I like the outlineless thing I did for Faye's flashbacks.

Pintsize should just do that at the end of EVERY comic.

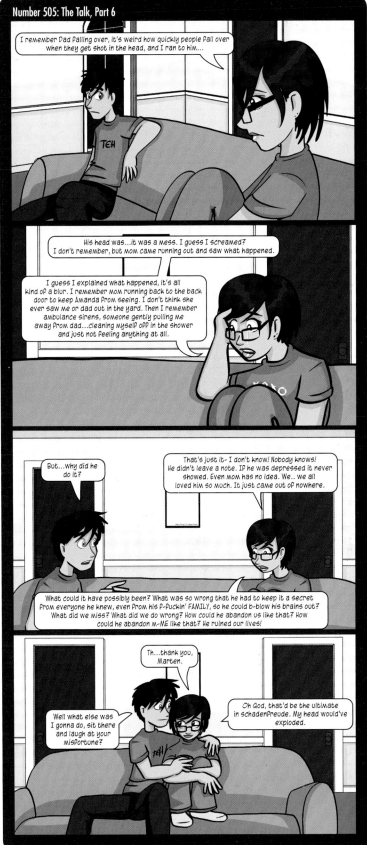

...

By this point my inbox was almost literally ON FIRE.

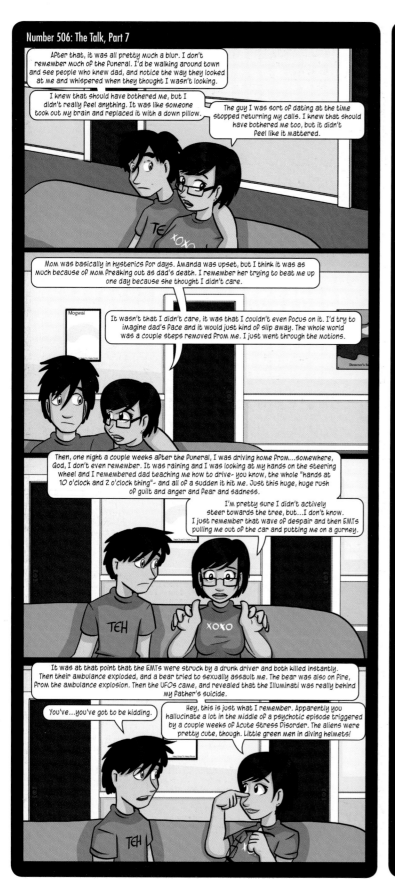

After that, it was all pretty much a blur. I don't remember much of the funeral. I'd be walking around town and see people who knew dad, and notice the way they looked at me and whispered when they thought I wasn't looking.

I knew that should have bothered me, but I didn't really feel anything. It was like someone took out my brain and replaced it with a down pillow.

The guy I was sort of dating at the time stopped returning my calls. I knew that should have bothered me too, but it didn't feel like it mattered.

Mom was basically in hysterics for days. Amanda was upset, but I think it was as much because of mom freaking out as dad's death. I remember her trying to beat me up one day because she thought I didn't care.

It wasn't that I didn't care, it was that I couldn't even focus on it. I'd try to imagine dad's face and it would just kind of slip away. The whole world was a couple steps removed from me. I just went through the motions.

Then, one night a couple weeks after the funeral, I was driving home from...somewhere, God, I don't even remember. It was raining and I was looking at my hands on the steering wheel and I remembered dad teaching me how to drive- you know, the whole "hands at 10 o'clock and 2 o'clock thing"- and all of a sudden it hit me. Just this huge, huge rush of guilt and anger and fear and sadness.

I'm pretty sure I didn't actively steer towards the tree, but...I don't know. I just remember that wave of despair and then EMTs pulling me out of the car and putting me on a gurney.

It was at that point that the EMTs were struck by a drunk driver and both killed instantly. Then their ambulance exploded, and a bear tried to sexually assault me. The bear was also on fire, from the ambulance explosion. Then the UFOs came, and revealed that the Illuminati was really behind my father's suicide.

You've...you've got to be kidding.

Hey, this is just what I remember. Apparently you hallucinate a lot in the middle of a psychotic episode triggered by a couple weeks of Acute Stress Disorder. The aliens were pretty cute, though. Little green men in diving helmets!

In hindsight, I probably should've spaced out this text more as flashbacks. But I remember being DESPERATE to get past the drama and back to jokes at this point.

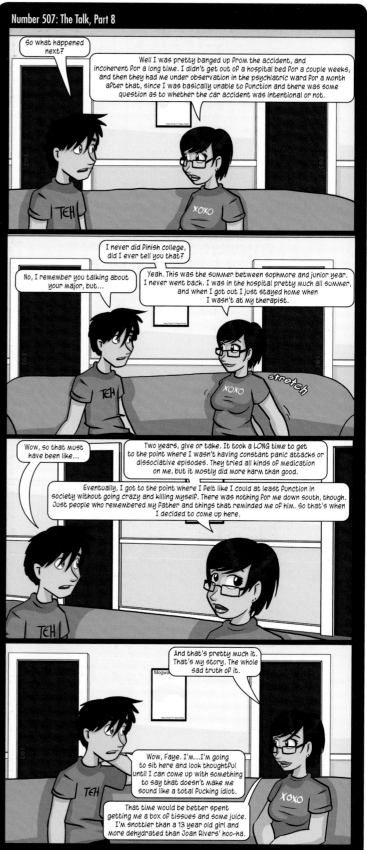

So what happened next?

Well I was pretty banged up from the accident, and incoherent for a long time. I didn't get out of a hospital bed for a couple weeks, and then they had me under observation in the psychiatric ward for a month after that, since I was basically unable to function and there was some question as to whether the car accident was intentional or not.

I never did finish college, did I ever tell you that?

No, I remember you talking about your major, but...

Yeah. This was the summer between sophmore and junior year. I never went back. I was in out pretty much all summer, and when I got out I just stayed home when I wasn't at my therapist.

Wow, so that must have been like...

Two years, give or take. It took a LONG time to get to the point where I wasn't having constant panic attacks or dissociative episodes. They tried all kinds of medication on me, but it mostly did more harm than good.

Eventually, I got to the point where I felt like I could at least function in society without going crazy and killing myself. There was nothing for me down south, though. Just people who remembered my father and things that reminded me of him. So that's when I decided to come up here.

And that's pretty much it. That's my story. The whole sad truth of it.

Wow, Faye. I'm...I'm going to sit here and look thoughtful until I can come up with something to say that doesn't make me sound like a total fucking idiot.

That time would be better spent getting me a box of tissues and some juice. I'm snottier than a 13 year old girl and more dehydrated than Joan Rivers' hoo-ha.

Apologies to Ms. Rivers.

104

MORE LIKE PRO BONER LOL

It's cool, they both just ended up going to sleep right away.

105

but Pintsize you do not have hips

FURIOUS PUNCHINGS

This is basically the only reason to go drinking at 1pm.

But…who took the picture? Did he set up a tripod?

Faye would not appreciate the Moby Dick comparison.

Believe it or not, this blonde girl will eventually become far and away the most popular character in the comic. Also her personality will be completely different.

Raven is COMPLETELY a lady.

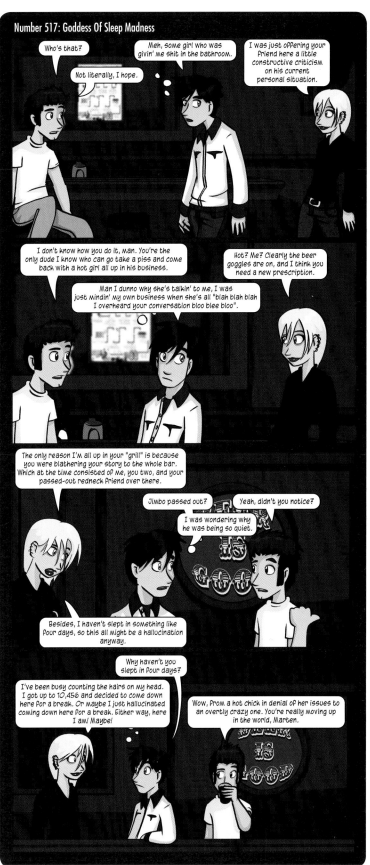

I still get people asking why Hannelore was so different in these early comics. She was on some really hardcore medication at the time. I TOTALLY WAS NOT JUST FIGURING HER OUT AS I WENT ALONG

NURRRRR

That waitress has EXCELLENT timing.

Spoiler warning: Hannelore totally murders Marten in the end.

Murmule is a pretty great word to say out loud.

Dora apparently irradiated his family.

The second one is definitely weirder.

Holy crap 2-point perspective in panel 2!

Spoiler warning: Marten is pretty apathetic about the whole "getting murdered" thing.

Number 526: It Is Dictionary Week

Language is fluid, Dora

Number 527: Those Poor Horsies

It took me FOREVER to come up with the design for an Apple-based AnthroPC. In hindsight it should've been really obvious.

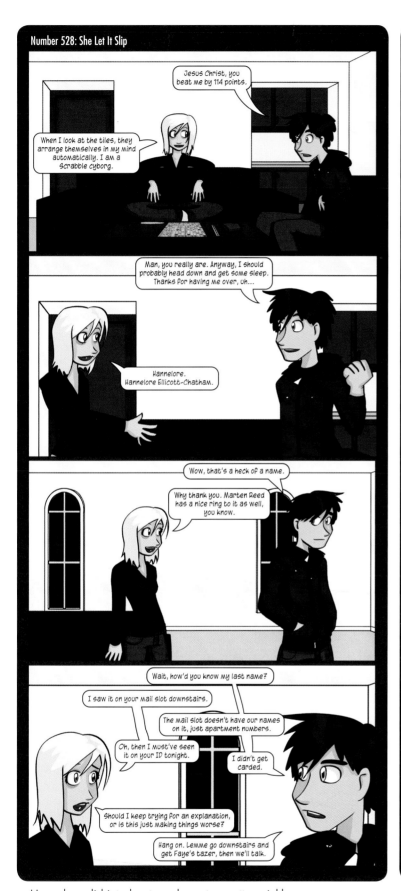

Hannelore slid into her true character pretty quickly.

That's right, I was doing taser jokes WAY before that stupid "don't taze me bro" meme.

Raven has had like FOURTEEN Shirley Temples.

Wait where is the taser now OH GOD PINTSIZE HAS IT D:

If metaphors were lead, this book would weigh 300 pounds.

Pintsize veers dangerously close to the fourth wall.

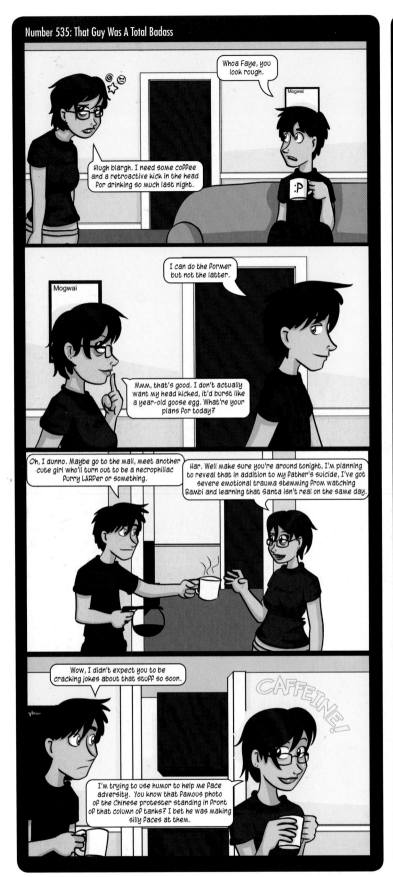

It's sad, and freaky, that we still don't know what happened to that guy.

Sexy traps can also be set using lingerie, a stick, and a cardboard box.

"Love in an Elevator" is ACTUALLY about the Nixon presidency and Watergate scandal.

kitty butt *

Number 539: Quick Thinking

Number 540: Utensils Of Doom

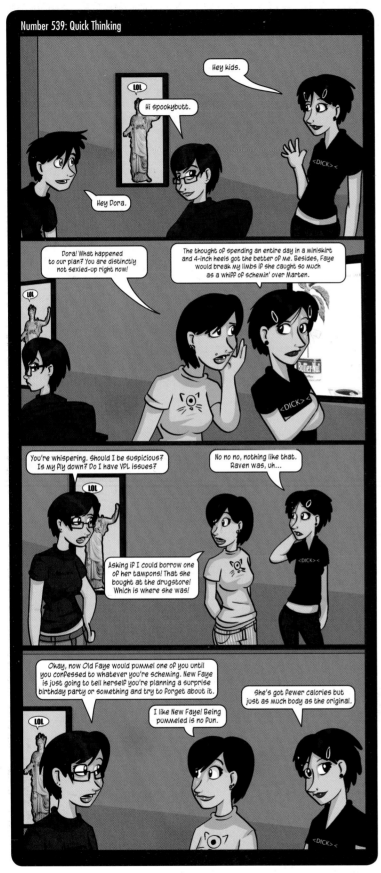

DICKFISH

Seriously, no coffee shop is complete without one.

Better than a horny Lucky the Leprechaun.

That's Raven's most popular line ever, in panel 4.

Never leave home without breath mints and a helmet.

Raven NOBODY should say "J/K LOL" out loud.

Number 545: Conversational

Dr. Raleigh Hobard-Cumberton, Professor of Piracy

Number 546: Arbitrarily Titled Strip

Pintsize better not ever get his hands on that doll.

Number 548: Belle And Sebitchslap?

www.sexybellowsbitches.com

It doesn't have genitalia, but it does have a working digestive tract.

I saw part of a Girls Gone Wild video once. It was actually really depressing :\

Q: How many indie rock snobs does it take to screw in a lightbulb?
A: psh, you use LIGHTBULBS?

That's called "doin' it Akira-style."

For those of you wondering what Pintsize's voice sounds like, now you know: it sounds like a TR-808 drum machine.

A sweaty, itchy gorilla.

I still record songs under the Deathmøle moniker.

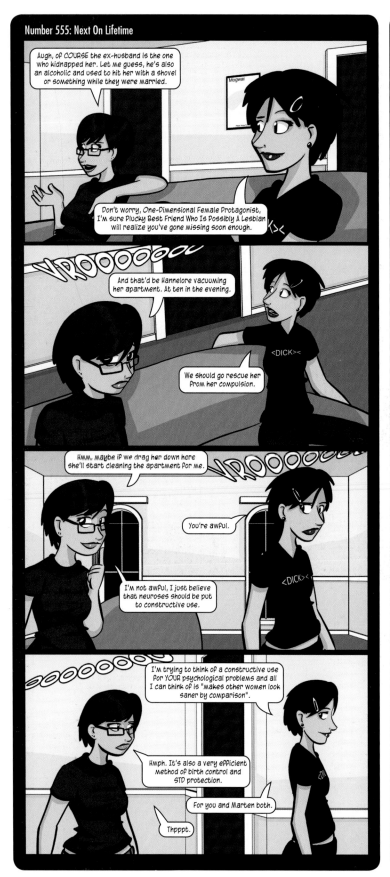

Good lord what is going on with Faye's hips in that last panel?

Wait, why isn't she wearing eye protection?!

128

Aww, look at that adorable bull! He's got dalmatian spots!

Who's lookin' at the bull? I'M busy ogling cute cowboy bottoms.

"Cowboy Bottoms"? I think I've seen that porn before.

So Hannelore, can I get the number for your therapist? I meant to ask you earlier but you skedaddled before I could.

Oh, sure. You'll like her, she's really nice.

Oh my god, did the announcer really just say "Git 'r done" unironically?

I'm not sure if I need someone really nice or someone willing to kick me in the ass and tell me to stop being so crazy.

Oh don't worry, my therapist can be tough when she needs to be.

Put up a sign for that in the coffeeshop and there'd be a line around the block.

Back when I was REALLY bad, she used to squirt me with a water pistol if she caught me counting the books in her bookcase or alphabetizing the magazines on her coffee table.

Hmm, hydrophobia instead of intimacy issues? Sounds like a fair trade to me.

"It kisses the boy or it gets the hose again." I like it!

Buffalo Bill was not a popular cognitive behavioral therapist.

Ooh, horn to the balls! That bull is totally going to get high-fives from his buddies back in the corral.

Ssh, I think Hannelore fell asleep.

Aww. We'd better let her be. She looks like she's been awake for days.

Yeah, she's got that whole Night of the Living Dead thing going. Speaking of going, I think it's time I headed home and got some rest myself.

Aww, you're not gonna stick around until Marty gets home?

Nah, I need teh sleepzorz. Grab his ass for me when he comes in.

Don't you think that'd be kind of mixed signals coming from me?

You? Sending mixed signals to Marten? Perish the thought.

Do you think the sound of me slapping that smirk off your face would wake Hannelore?

It'd probably be pretty loud, so yeah.

129

THE GAME'S AFOOT

He could just scribble it on with a Sharpie or something, I guess.

RIP Steve Irwin :(

The dues are very reasonable and if you ever want to drop out of the club we promise it won't hurt our feelings, just tell us in advance, okay?

131

Brrr. It's getting chilly out.

Do you, uh, want my hoodie?

Nah, I'll be okay.

So, uh, here's your apartment...

I'm pretty wired from all that coffee. Are you tired?

No, not really. I did have like six cokes.

Well, let's go up on the roof. It's got a nice view.

Oh yeah? But won't you be cold?

Maybe, but I can just gut you and climb inside your carcass to keep warm.

Oh, of course. That way you won't have to do something rash, like going all the way down to your apartment and getting a sweater.

Cashmere is comfy, but it just can't compare with steaming human entrails.

Try telling THAT to human-rights activists. "Steaming human entrails are murder!" they yell, all throwin' ketchup on your brand-new intestine jacket.

They're not murder if you just FOUND them like that.

132

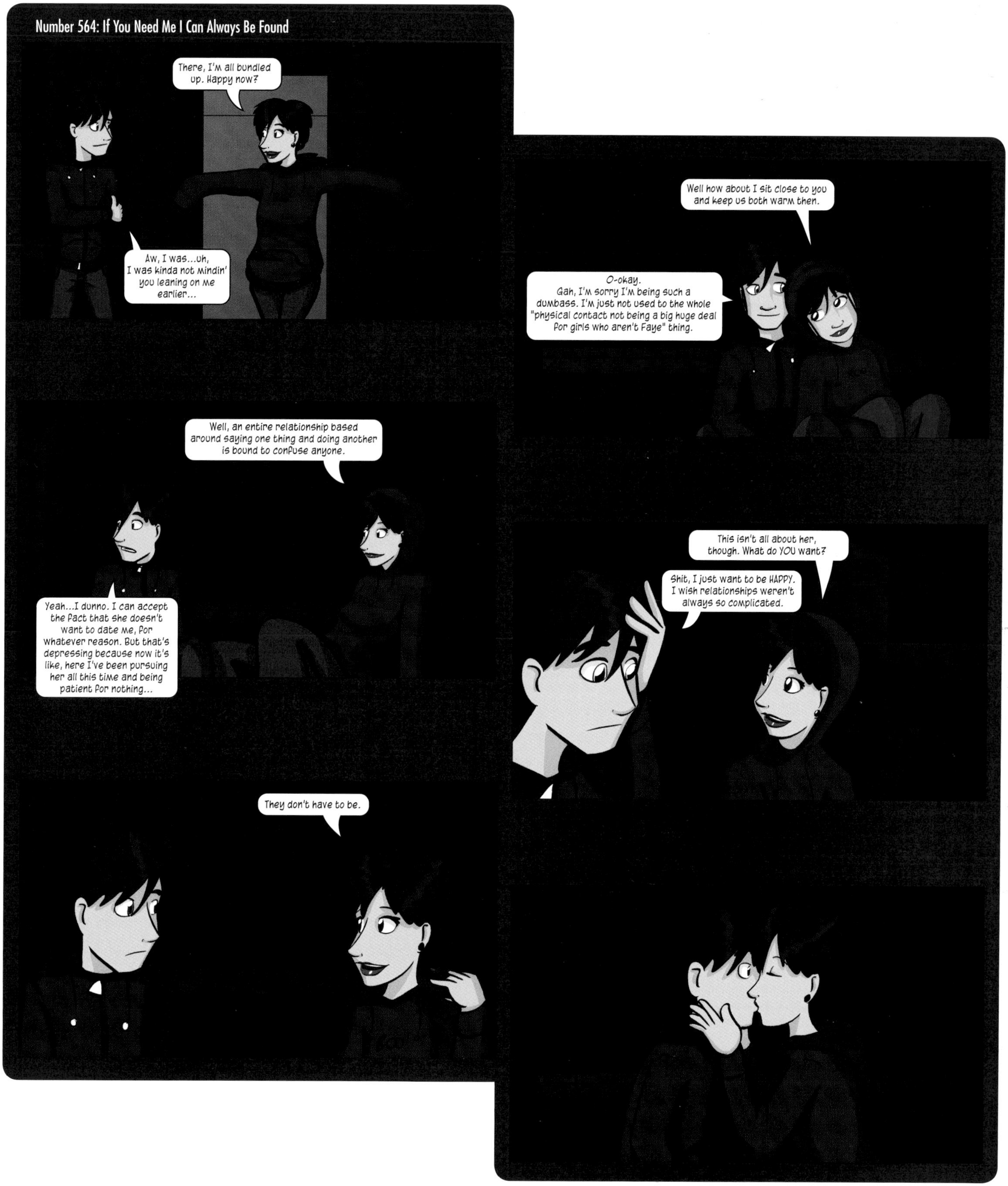
Number 564: If You Need Me I Can Always Be Found
There, I'm all bundled up. Happy now?
Aw, I was...uh, I was kinda not mindin' you leaning on me earlier...
Well how about I sit close to you and keep us both warm then.
O-okay. Gah, I'm sorry I'm being such a dumbass. I'm just not used to the whole "physical contact not being a big huge deal for girls who aren't Faye" thing.
Well, an entire relationship based around saying one thing and doing another is bound to confuse anyone.
Yeah...I dunno. I can accept the fact that she doesn't want to date me, for whatever reason. But that's depressing because now it's like, here I've been pursuing her all this time and being patient for nothing...
This isn't all about her, though. What do YOU want?
Shit, I just want to be HAPPY. I wish relationships weren't always so complicated.
They don't have to be.

OMG KISSES :O

Wouldn't they be cold, clammy necrophilia makeouts?

And also we can convert matter directly into energy and travel through time. Didn't you know?

Italo-Swede sounds like a kind of dance music I would enjoy.

DRAMA DRAMA DRAMA DRAMA

135

Number 569: Cocoa Is A Good Peace Offering

Take a moment and think about it: odds are, your mom has done blowjobs to people. YOU'RE WELCOME

Number 570: She Missed It All

Whoa, skinny line-art in panel 1! This was an experiment at the time, but it's pretty close to the line weight I use these days too.

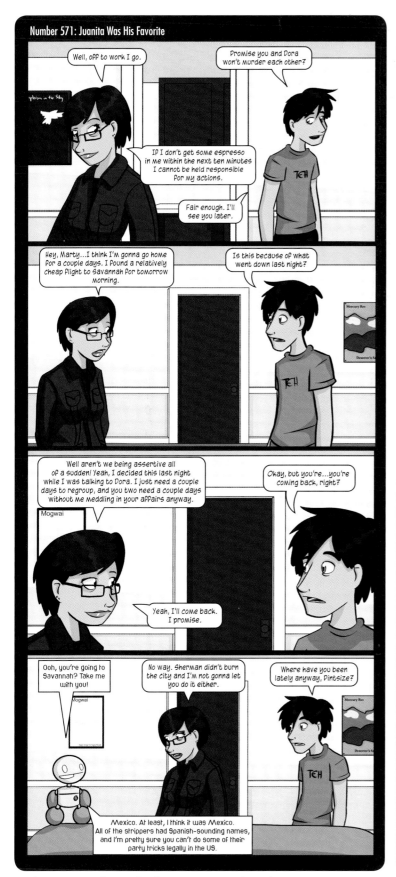

Their party tricks involved voting in Canadian elections.

Definitely human shield.

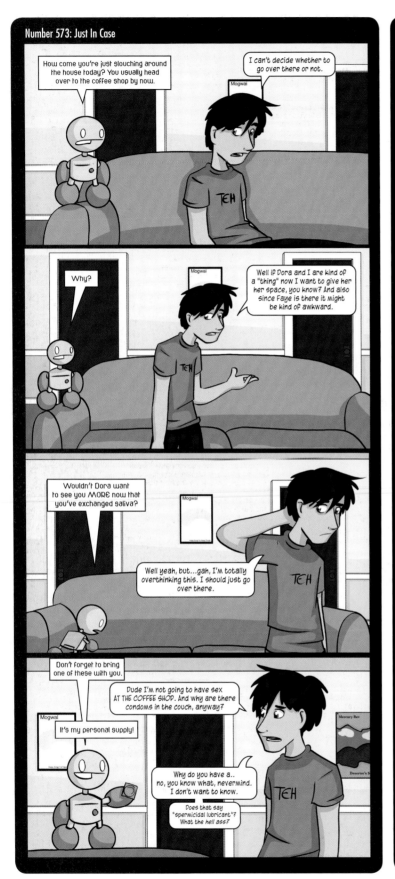

Number 573: Just In Case

You know, so he doesn't knock anyone up.

Number 574: A Common Fantasy

I have it on good authority it's more like 3/4 the female population of Manhattan.

It's either The Smile or he just ate a bunch of Vicodin!

Genghis Khan would've burned entire villages over Faye.

Number 577: The Dallas Cop-Out

This is all really a dream, but it's HANNELORE'S dream, not Marten's.

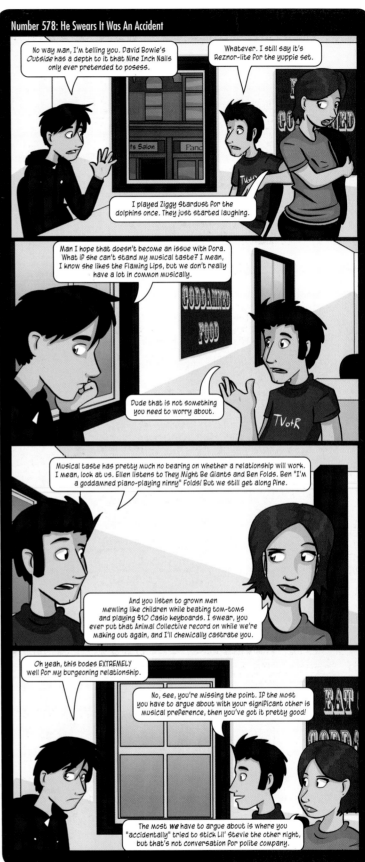

Number 578: He Swears It Was An Accident

He tried to stick Lil' Stevie in her armpit. It was…it was weird.

I had a friend in college who broke her girlfriend's pelvis while they were having private-times. I was like, "wow."

Do some vocal warmups, avoid sugary drinks that day, etc.

RIP Wesley Willis :(

SERIOUSLY NOT HELPFUL RAVEN >:|

Old Spice and aftershave: Dadsmells™.

This is why they don't do 1-hour adoption services in Las Vegas.

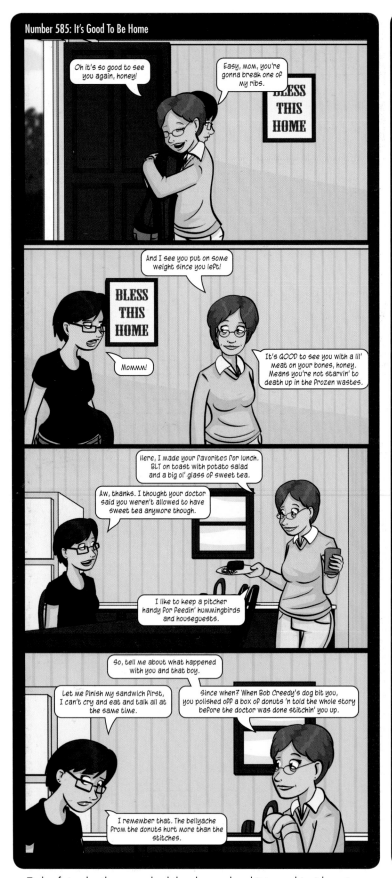

To be fair, she then punched the dog so hard it turned inside out and burst into flames.

I still think Mastodon and the Decemberists would be a pretty good double-billing.

Number 587: Parental Hypocrisy

...And th-that's the huh-whole story. Now Marty and Dora are to-together and I'm left in the lu-lurch.

Oh honey, I knew it was gonna end badly soon as you told me you were livin' with that boy. I'm sorry it happened, though.

I know I did the right thing in the end. I mean, it really hurts, but at least everythin'll work out for the best. Marten and Dora don't hate me, and I'm gonna start goin' to therapy, and life'll go on, right?

Of course it will honey, that's life's blessin'. It always goes on.

Y'know, I was in a similar situation with your daddy and another girl, when we were young.

Yeah, but you ended up marryin' dad. How'd you get him to pick you instead of the other girl?

Oh, that was easy. I just put out first.

Mom!

Well I didn't say it was EXACTLY like your situation!

When in doubt, put out first.

Number 588: Shrinkage

Well I'm glad you're gettin' back into therapy, honey. It's what got you back on your feet after that accident. I don't know why you ever stopped goin' in the first place.

Ugh, I dunno. I just wasn't ready to deal with all that stuff, y'know? But now I'm just tired of NOT dealin' with it. I'd rather get it over with.

What about you, mom? Seeing a shrink would probably do you some good.

Oh you know I don't like that sort of thing. I go to church, I keep myself busy, and that's enough for me.

I'm glad you've come to terms with Amanda being gay, at least.

Well I don't APPROVE of it, but you know Amanda. She's gonna get her way, one way or another. 'Sides, it's not like it's hurtin' anything, other'n my chances of seein' grand-children someday.

No offense mom, but I don't see Amanda with kids no matter WHICH team she bats for.

I know, but look at the alternative. I love you, sweetie, but you're crazier than a mule on a Ferris wheel.

Poor mule. He doesn't know how he got up there, but he's sure as hell gonna bite the first person who tries to get him down.

Hahahaha oh man I had forgotten about that simile, I think that is one of my better ones.

Why, the Lord Jesus Christ checks, OBVIOUSLY.

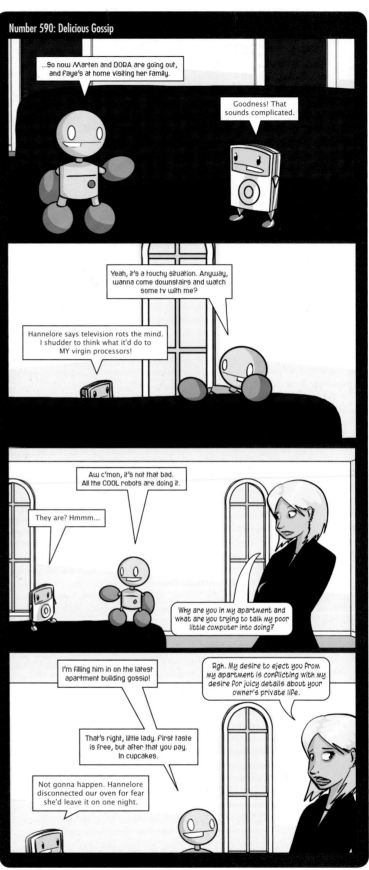

I have left the oven on overnight before :(

Also that would've been pretty expensive to have engraved on the tombstone.

Aw geez Dora

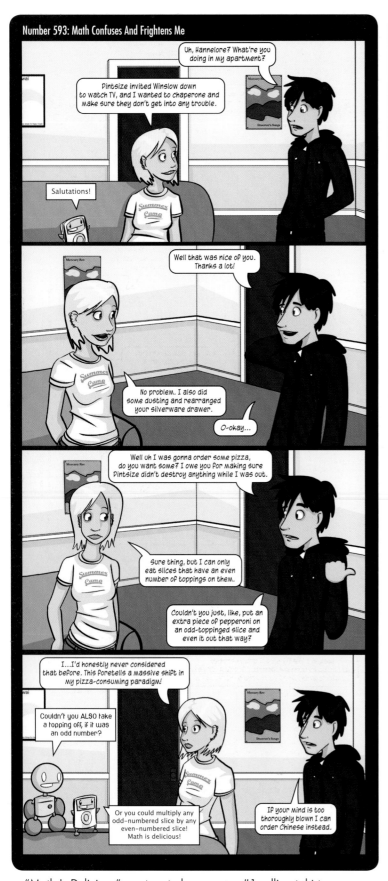

Number 593: Math Confuses And Frightens Me

"Math Is Delicious" went on to become my #1 selling t-shirt of all time.

Number 594: He Has An Awesome Van

The Makeout Hobo was based on a real person. He crashed on my couch for a few weeks. Then the cops ran him out of town. This actually happened.

No, no, she's been turning SKATEBOARD tricks. She's really good at skateboarding!

Hannelore did not actually go to college.

Number 597: Tomato Plants Are Fun To Draw

Either one is a viable option!

Number 598: Safety First

...But what if the dachshund is riding a really fast horse?

Aw yeah, ending this volume with a fart joke. KEEP IT CLASSY, QUESTIONABLE CONTENT.

Guest Comics & Bonus Art

The following is a selection of guest strips that I've done for other artists, as well as miscellaneous sketches and other drawings, generally from around the same time as the comics collected in this volume. Enjoy!

J. Jacques (with apologies to Mitch Clem)   WWW.NOTHINGNICE.COM

DIESEL SWEETIES (C) RSTEVENS
GUEST STRIP BY J.JACQUES (QUESTIONABLECONTENT.NET)

ABOVE: Overcompensating is my friend/publisher/overlord Jeffrey's fake journal comic that is also real.

OPPOSITE, UPPER LEFT: I did this as a random little doodle for a website called Ban Comic Sans. It's still circulating on the internet, years later. Weird.

OPPOSITE, LOWER LEFT: Nothing Nice To Say was, along with Scary Go Round, the defining influence for QC. It showed that you could do a smart, funny comic about music culture.

OPPOSITE, RIGHT: Diesel Sweeties was either the first or second webcomic I ever read (I can't remember). Doing a guest strip for RStevens was definitely a "holy shit, I made it" moment.

Hate Song was one of the most delightfully twisted webcomics around, back in the day. My guest strip was actually relatively TAME compared to their regular strips.

I still think "The Adventures of Garfield and Goku" would be an EXCELLENT comic.

Guest strip by J. Jacques of questionablecontent.net

Ever since I first started reading Dinosaur Comics, I've always thought T-Rex's ankle looked really fucked up in that last panel. So I decided to address the issue in my guest strip.

I think we can all agree that a newspaper-syndicated version of QC would be uniformly terrible.

Sam and Fuzzy was the very first "established" comic to ever link to QC, and Sam Logan has become a good friend of mine over the years.

LEFT: Sam Logan is, however, also a horrific degenerate beast of a man who will not hesitate to punch a granny or give a puppy cancer.

ABOVE: These are the first drawings I ever did of Hannelore, back before I even knew who she was or whether she'd ever appear in the comic.

There was a "laser portraits" meme going around the internet, and I decided it would be funny to do some of the characters' high-school photos using that backdrop.

Afterword

I remember very clearly the day I decided to reveal what happened to Faye's dad. My wife and I were down in Tennessee visiting her family. I woke up early one morning and said to myself "okay, I've been dancing around the Marten and Faye will-they-won't-they issue for too long. Time to address it." So I sat down and wrote ten comics in about 45 minutes. Those scripts would, after only minor changes, become "The Talk," the series of comics starting at number 500 in this collection and online.

The decision wasn't entirely spur-of-the-moment; I had known for a while that Faye's big secret would be her father's suicide. But I had initially imagined this big reveal wouldn't happen until the end of the comic, after which she and Marten would presumably get together and live happily ever after.

I had put myself in an awkward situation, though—the comic was extremely successful, and was in fact my full-time job. I didn't want to end the strip, because I was having way too much fun making it, and I didn't want to put myself out of work. So I did the only thing I could think of: I took things in the opposite direction. Marten and Faye WOULDN'T get together after the big reveal. Hopefully this would generate enough other ideas that I could keep the comic interesting for me and my readers.

In the meantime, though, I had to ACTUALLY DO THE COMICS. Oh God. I was TERRIFIED that I was wrecking my comic, destroying my livelihood, ruining my life. But I had no choice.

So I started putting up the comics. And my inbox exploded.

Emails from folks who'd lost family members or friends or spouses to suicide. People who had attempted suicide themselves, or suffered from depression and suicidal thoughts. Readers who hadn't gone through anything like that, but who were nevertheless profoundly affected. I was flabbergasted. I knew I was going to provoke a reaction with these strips, but not to this extent. To see it touch so many people on such a personal level was utterly unexpected.

The most poignant message I received was from a reader with a daughter of his own. He was depressed, and had been seriously considering suicide. But when he read those comics, he realized that he didn't want to put his daughter through anything like Faye had endured, and decided to get help.

I didn't set out to make some sort of Grand Statement, or Change People's Lives, or anything like that. I was just trying to tell the best story I could. But knowing I've helped people, and maybe even saved some lives, is the greatest and most humbling affirmation of my work I could ever hope to receive.

RATED THE #1 COMICS IN THE WORLD
BY PEOPLE WHO LIE ABOUT STATISTICS

OVERCOMPENSATING
by **Jeffrey J. Rowland**

Overcompensating is the almost 100% true journal comic of cowboy-poet/hacker/CEO/amateur electrician Jeffrey Rowland, who happens to harbor a seething disdain for reality. There is a person in it called Weedmaster P and a green cat that is maybe a zombie.

books: **topatoco.com/wigu**
read online: **overcompensating.com**

SAM & FUZZY
by **Sam Logan**

Gangster gerbils looting your cellar? Stalker vampires getting in your space? Don't panic! Ninja Mafia Services is here to help, with all the resources a near-bankrupt ex-crime-syndicate has to offer. (None.) So relax—and let *Sam & Fuzzy* fix your problem.

books: **topatoco.com/samandfuzzy**
read online: **samandfuzzy.com**

WONDERMARK
by **David Malki !**

A sarcastic, silly, and razor-sharp gag comic strip created entirely from 19th-Century woodcuts, this Eisner-, Harvey-, and Ignatz-nominated comic is in equal measures strange, attractive, clever and good-natured—*just like you.*

books: **topatoco.com/wondermark**
read online: **wondermark.com**

NEDROID PICTURE DIARY
by **Anthony Clark**

Beartato is a bear who is also a potato. His best friend is a bird-man. Sometimes there is a walking shark or a mean dog. Don't worry! This is almost entirely made-up.

books: **topatoco.com/nedroid**
read online: **nedroid.com**

THE ADVENTURES OF DR. McNINJA
by **Christopher Hastings**

He's the doctor who cured Paul Bunyan's Disease, the disease that turns you into a giant lumberjack. He's the ninja who defeated the raptor-riding Mexican bandits, and gained a mustachioed 12-year-old sidekick in the process. He's a man who encounters an above-average amount of explosions. He's Dr. McNinja.

books: **topatoco.com/raptorbandit**
read online: **drmcninja.com**

A SOFTER WORLD
by **Joey Comeau & Emily Horne**

A Softer World comics are like a weird sad clown that lives under your bed. Except the tears are blood. And when the clown coughs, the most adorable kitten in the world pops out of his mouth and loves you.

books: **topatoco.com/asofterworld**
read online: **asofterworld.com**

DINOSAUR COMICS
by **Ryan North**

Dinosaur Comics is a comic about dinosaurs and friendly good times! It stars T-Rex, who likes to stomp on things such as houses and cars and humans, and Utahraptor, who likes to tell T-Rex that this is not such a good idea. It uses the same pictures in every comic with just the words changed! It is Better Than It Sounds.

books: **topatoco.com/qwantz**
read online: **qwantz.com**

THE ANIME CLUB
by **KC Green**

Four kids on a journey through friendship and back. The Anime Club kids are notorious for being not well liked around the library or the school, but that's okay 'cause they got each other. OR DO THEY? Sorta. It goes back and forth. Collecting parts 1–5 of the entire saga and plenty of extra material to pop your buttons. GET A BIB.

books: **topatoco.com/rumblo**
read online: **gunshowcomic.com**

AMAZINGSUPERPOWERS
by **Wes Citti & Tony Wilson**

What do radioactive goats piloting bomber jets, infants irreedeem-ably infatuated with 1970s game-show hosts, and sentient valve cover gaskets have in common? None of them are in this book! At least, I don't think so. *Dare you find out for yourself?*

books: **topatoco.com/asp**
read online: **amazingsuperpowers.com**

DRESDEN CODAK
by **Aaron Diaz**

Housing piles of exclusive art, timelines, background information and comic theory, as well as a 7 page opener to "Dark Science", the *Dresden Codak Primer* is an indispensable resource for both longtime fans and a superb introduction to new ones. How have you lived your life without it? Probably *badly.*

books: **topatoco.com/dc**
read online: **dresdencodak.com**

ALL THESE FINE ITEMS AND MANY MORE PUZZLING ONES AT
TOPATOCO.COM